Faith Out Loud

A Cumberland Presbyterian
YOUTH RESOURCE
Volume 2, Quarter 1

Discipleship Ministry Team
Ministry Council
Cumberland Presbyterian Church

Fall 2012

8207 Traditional Place
Cordova (Memphis), Tennessee 38016

©2012 Discipleship Ministry Team

All Rights Reserved. No part of this book may be reproduced or transmitted in any form or by any means, electronic or mechanical, including photocopying, recording, or by any information storage or retrieval system, without permission in writing from the publisher with the single exception that purchase of this curriculum grants the purchaser the right to copy and distribute student handouts within each lesson for use in their local church. For information address Discipleship Ministry Team, Cumberland Presbyterian Center, 8207 Traditional Place, Cordova (Memphis), Tennessee, 38016-7414.

The Discipleship Ministry Team of the Ministry Council of the Cumberland Presbyterian Church is the successor organization to the Board of Christian Education of the Cumberland Presbyterian Church.

Funded, in part, by your contributions to Our United Outreach.

First Edition 2012

Published by The Discipleship Ministry Team, CPC
Memphis, Tennessee

ISBN-13: 978-0615681221
ISBN-10: 0615681220

We want to hear from you.
Please send your comments about this curriculum to
the Discipleship Ministry Team at faithoutloud@cumberland.org

OUR UNITED OUTREACH
Made Possible In Part By Your Tithe To Our United Outreach

Table of Contents

Curriculum Users Guide. v

Lesson 1: And God Said. 1

Lesson 2: The Fall. 11

Lesson 3: Cain and Able. 23

Lesson 4: The Flood.. 33

Lesson 5: The Tower of Babel.. 43

Lesson 6: The Sacrifice: Issac. 55

Lesson 7: Sibling Rivalry. 67

Lesson 8: Revenge to Reconciliation. 85

Lesson 9: Plagues and Passover. 93

Lesson 10: The Original Pretty Woman. 109

Lesson 11: My God Rules, your god Drools.. 113

Lesson 12: It's About Love, Not a Big Fish. 121

Lesson 13: Is 2012 the End?. 143

Welcome to the Faith Out Loud curriculum!

It is our prayer that these lessons both encourage you and equip you as a youth leader—we're so grateful for what you do in the lives of students!

Blessings to you and your ministry!

Below are explanations of the components found in each lesson and tips for using this curriculum.

Lesson Title: Each lesson has a catchy title. Use these titles as teasers to get your students excited about upcoming gatherings.

Scripture: Each lesson has a key scripture reference. Spend some time studying and praying through each week's passage as you prepare to teach.

Theme: The theme statement gives you a quick snapshot into the main point of the lesson.

Before The Lesson: This section is usually divided into two parts: *Resource List* and *Leader Prep*. *Resource List* give you a quick list of all the stuff you need to gather for each week. *Leader Prep* give detailed instructions on the advance work that needs to be done for that week's activities. Do NOT wait until the night before you teach to review this section.

The Lesson: Once you move into the teaching time, you'll see these recurring elements:
- ✓ **Get Started:** These activities are designed to draw students into the material and set up the theme for the lesson.
- ✓ **Discussion Questions:** Usually a group of open-ended questions, these moments in the lesson are strategically placed to encourage your students to both think about and respond to the topic at hand.
- ✓ **Explain:** Placed in *italics*, these sections can be read verbatim to your students to help them fully understand the implications of the topic or theme. You'll discover you'll get the best response when you are thoroughly familiar with these sections and can deliver the same information in your own words instead of just reading the info to the students.
- ✓ **Leader Tips:** You'll find sections of side notes throughout each lesson. These are notes just for you, the leader. These notes offer you everything from instructions on how to facilitate the activities to background information on the subject to tips in making your lesson run smoothly.
- ✓ **Listen Up:** This section highlights a key scripture passage that should be read aloud. Encourage student to do these readings as often as possible.
- ✓ **Now What:** This section helps your students respond to the lesson. This will drive the lesson home and get your students thinking about the lesson in terms outside of the classroom walls.
- ✓ **Live It:** This is simply just the closing of each lesson, designed to help you conclude your time with your students well and offer them something to think about in the week ahead. Most weeks have handouts to pass along to your students during this time. You may find it helpful to encourage your students to get a folder to keep these handouts together so they can easily refer to them during the week.
- ✓ **Handouts:** At the end of each week's lesson, you'll find a reproducible page. Your purchase of this curriculum grants you the right to print and distribute copies to everyone in your group.

Leader Tip:
The words used in the creation story are interesting. Adam is spelled just like — but pronounced differently than—the Hebrew word for dirt/earth and man/humankind. That's why, throughout the first two chapters of Genesis, some translations say Adam and some say the man. Eve is very much like the Hebrew word for life or provider of life. Eden means delight.

tempt students to agree with your position instead of thinking the matter through for themselves, or turn this lesson into an argument.

Be aware that regardless of your geographic location or local ethos, your students have been raised in a culture that is saturated with the message that the universe and life just happened. The goal of this lesson is to instill within your students an appreciation for God's gift of creation and God as Creator.

Explaining the Bible

The word *genesis* means beginning, so it's appropriate that the Bible begins with a book called Genesis, and it is equally appropriate that within this book is the story of the beginning of everything we know. The title of Genesis comes from the Latin translation (done around A.D. 400) of the Greek translation (done around 250 B.C.) of the first words of the Bible, originally written in Hebrew (maybe in 1450 B.C. or so), "In the beginning."

Almost every culture throughout history has had its own story about how the world began. What we have in Genesis is the story as found in the Hebrew culture. Moses is said to have written Genesis as the first part of the Pentateuch. The Pentateuch is the first five books of the Bible. Presumably, though, Moses had to rely on oral or possibly written accounts of events which occurred before his lifetime, and someone else wrote the account of his death in Deuteronomy 34.

Some Christians believe creation happened exactly as it's told in Genesis, and some of these folks seem to think that saying anything else calls the truthfulness of the whole Bible into doubt. Other Christians believe that the creation account in Genesis is how ancient Hebrews made sense of what they couldn't comprehend. Such Christians might say that the creation story in Genesis doesn't have to be 100% scientifically accurate to convey the truth that God is the Creator.

Science says something happened billions of years ago that caused a big bang, and that bang created the universe, then something else happened and life began. That is, of course, an over-simplification of two well-developed scientific theories. The Bible, on the other hand, says God created the universe and everything in it…by speaking. Voice is a powerful force in the Judeo-Christian tradition. God spoke creation into existence. The Exodus began with a conversation between Moses and God. The Law was spoken by God.

And God Said...
by Andy McClung

Scripture: Genesis 1:1-2:3

Theme: God created everything. Creation reveals God's glory, power, wisdom, beauty, goodness, and love.

Resource List

- Varied arts supplies, including clay or play-dough
- CD of nature sounds
- Music player (laptop, iPod, MP3 player, CD player, speakers, etc.)
- A bucket or bag containing strips of paper with words written on them (optional)

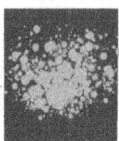

Leader Prep

- Have a CD of nature sounds playing softly throughout this lesson.
- Select a spot outdoors for the conclusion of this lesson or, better yet, the whole lesson.
- Prepare strips of paper with the words to build a poem. Some suggested words to include in the bag are: sunset, smell, falling, fuzzy, pretty, feathers, beach, moon, mountain, tree, blue, green, bloom, the, cloud, clear, sky, summer, over, under, fall, spring, winter, snow, gently, waves, sand, fur, antler, ears, bounding, flower, leaf, leaves, branches, shining, grass, waving, breeze, soar, wings, roots, every, beautiful, your, God, amazing, colors, deep, fill, show, bursting, walk, always, every, never, can't, will, why, and...

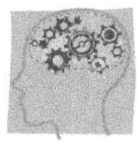

Leader Insight

Connecting to Your Students
Teens wonder whether or not creation happened exactly as described in Genesis. This lesson acknowledges the controversy between Creationism and the Big Bang/Evolution Theory, but doesn't seek to solve that debate. As you teach, take care in expressing your position in the controversy, even though your students will probably ask. Strongly staking a claim on either side of the debate may reduce your influence on students who are leaning toward the opposite side,

Leader Tip:
Darwin published his book on evolution in 1859. The Big Bang Theory developed in the 1920s and 30s, but wasn't given that name until 1950.

happens without controlling every tiny detail of the universe.

Some Christians prefer to ignore all other theories about creation and "just believe what the Bible says." While that position is a great display of faith, it doesn't really help in conversing with people outside the church. Faith in God is a good thing, of course, and essential to Christian discipleship, but having the vocabulary and ability to discuss rationally such matters as the origins of the universe and life is important as well. Hopefully, this lesson will help your students do that.

Theological Underpinnings
There is room in Christianity and even in the Cumberland Presbyterian Church for people to have different ideas about how God created everything. To be Cumberland Presbyterian, however, one must agree that God was indeed behind creation in one way or another (*Confession of Faith* 1.10-1.12). A future FAITH OUT LOUD lesson will deal with our stewardship of creation, but this lesson focuses on God as Creator.

The opening activity will help students understand the difference between God's creation of everything and humans making things. It will also explore that humans have never created or destroyed any physical thing, but have only rearranged what God created. The Bible study portion of the lesson will inspire students to think of God as Creator, and might encourage them to make up their own minds about Creationism vs. Big Bang/Evolution rather than simply echo what they've heard others say. The responding and closing activities will solidify God as Creator in students' minds.

Applying the Lesson to Your Own Life
Some Christians welcome informed debate in the church, while some fear it. Which is your reaction? Why? Are there some matters where you welcome debate and other matters in which you fear debate? If so, what's the difference—in you—regarding the different matters?

What's your take on creation? Did God make everything out of nothing? Was it all just a random accident? Did God cause the big bang? Take a few moments and pretend you're actually on the opposite side of the debate. Which arguments and evidence would you find compelling? Which would you find ludicrous?

How much do you rely on God's creation every day? How much time do you spend with, or in, God's creation? How

God spoke to Samuel and to Jeremiah, and then they spoke for God to the people. Zechariah doubted God's messenger and lost his voice. Mary sang the Magnificat the first time she was recognized as being the mother of the Lord. John the Baptizer verbally announced the coming kingdom. Jesus resisted temptation by quoting scripture, exercised power over demons by speaking to them, and raised the dead with his words. Stephen's words got him martyred. Today we read scripture aloud in worship. Baptism and communion are sacraments only when the proper words are said, and the preacher speaks to the congregation to proclaim God's word. Yes, voice matters in our tradition.

In the discussion of the origin of the universe and life, many people see science and religion as opposite sides of the argument. Some Christians say they believe what the Bible says and anything else must be a lie. Some scientists take an equally hostile approach to the idea of God as Creator. For example, *Scientific American* ran an article in 2002 entitled "15 Answers to Creationist Nonsense," and has an online link to a special report that promises resources to "win all your debates against creationists." Many others on this same side of the debate refuse to consider any faith-based theory as valid. That's understandable, really. They've been trained to observe the natural world. God is supernatural.

Many Christians are just as combative in this debate. One thing Christians should bear in mind before launching into any attack, though, is that there are two kinds of evolution. One kind says that a species can evolve, or change, while remaining the same species. This idea does not seem to be in conflict with scripture. The other kind of evolution says that one species can evolve, or change, into another. This is the kind that says humans came from something else. This idea is far more difficult to reconcile with scripture.

In Ephesians 1:9-10 there is a hint of God having an overall plan for the universe. While Cumberland Presbyterians don't believe that God dictates everything that happens in the universe, we do believe that God knows everything that will happen. Creation was not accidental, but part of God's plan. Another part of the plan was human freedom. Just as God doesn't control every snake, bee, tornado, and breeze, God freely allows us to choose our own actions. God does, however, have a plan for us and hopes that we will listen, hear, and fulfill it. Creation, then, was not an accident. God did not set the universe in motion and then abandon it. God created everything, and in various ways is still involved in what

Notes:

often do you praise God as Creator? How often do you really thank God for creation?

The Lesson

Get Started (12 min.)

Creation

Direct students to the art supplies and tell them they each have five minutes to design a living thing that does not already exist. This thing cannot be a combination of already existing things, nor can it be a modified version of anything already in existence, real or fictional. It has to be something completely original. After five minutes, call time. This should be a nearly impossible task, but if anyone comes up with something, ask the rest of the class to judge whether or not it meets the criteria.

Discussion Question:
- What's the difference between making something and creating something?

Allow answers, but don't comment. Then explain: The first definition for *create* on dictionary.com is "to cause to come into being, as something unique that would not naturally evolve or that is not made by ordinary processes." The first definition for *make* is "to bring into existence by shaping or changing material, combining parts, etc."

Repeat or summarize those definitions if needed, and then ask students if they can agree to this statement: A creation has something of the creator in it. If you need to, give an example of this "something" as the creator's personality, hopes, dreams, fears, joy, emotional pain, etc. When everyone can agree to that statement, then say: If a creation has something of its creator in it, then we can know God—at least partially—by looking at what God created.

Notes:

Leader Tip:
Note that the first creation story is more compatible with our Confession of Faith, which says male and female were "created equal and complimentary" (1.11).

Listen Up (25 min.)

Have students read aloud Genesis 1:1–2:3, broken up as follows: 1:1-5, 1:6-8, 1:9-13, 1:14-19, 1:20-23, 1:24-31, and 2:1-3.

Discussion Question:
- When do you feel closest to God?

If no one mentions it, explain that a lot of people feel closest to God while in creation/nature. Most gods and idols ancient religions invented had something to do with nature. (For example: the Greek god of the sea was Poseidon, and the idol for the Egyptian god Sobek was a crocodile.) Humans have always associated nature with gods, or God. In the Old Testament there are people who encounter God in windstorms, clouds, and bushes. Isn't it odd, then, that nowadays we usually worship God—the creator of nature—inside buildings with opaque windows, completely closed off from nature? Many of us even have artificial plants in the sanctuary, as if real, God-made plants aren't good enough; or is it that we just don't care enough about creation to take care of real, living, plants in the sanctuary?

Discussion Questions:
- What in creation/nature makes you feel closest to God? Push every student to answer, especially if you plan to use the Respond activity "Creation, Round Two."
- Why do you think God spoke creation into existence (instead of, say, snapping fingers or just thinking)?
- According to the Bible verses we just read, what was God's opinion of creation?

If no one mentions it, point out that God saw that all creation was "good," but considered humankind "very good" (1:31).

Discussion Question:
- What does it mean to you that God saw creation as good and humankind as very good?

Move on to ask your students about the scripture they all read aloud just a few minutes ago.

Say: *Earlier we read about the creation of humankind, male and female, but no one read the names Adam and Eve because they don't appear as individuals in this story. They only appear in the second creation story, and (in some translations) aren't named until even later.*

Have someone read aloud Genesis 2:4-23.

Discussion Questions:
- What are some of the differences you notice between this story and the one we read a few minutes ago? Use the chart below if students need some help.

Genesis 1	Genesis 2 (and following)
Plants created on day 3, birds and fish on day 5, land animals on day 6, humans created last	God creates man before any plants or animals
Male and female created at the same time	The man is made first, then the woman
God addresses male and female together, as equals	The man seems to have power over the woman (for example: God makes her for him, and in 3:20 Adam names her)

Discussion Questions:
- Why do you think we have two creation stories in the Bible?
- What in the two stories is the same? Use the chart below if students need some help.

Genesis 1	Genesis 2
God created everything	God created everything
God created humankind a little more special than everything else ("very good")	God created humankind a little more special than everything else ("breath of life")

Discussion Questions:
- Do you think the Bible was meant to be read in the same way you'd read a science textbook? If so, which do you trust to be more factual? If not, what's the difference?
- Do you think the Bible spends more time explaining *how* God did stuff, or *why* God did stuff?

JUST IN CASE

If the discussion becomes too tense, try telling this joke.

A group of scientists got together and decided that science had advanced to the point that humankind no longer needed God. So they picked one scientist to go and tell God they were done with him.

The scientist walked up to God and said, "We just don't need you anymore. We can genetically engineer better food. We can clone animals and people. We can cure diseases. We can keep people alive longer. We can even create life from basic elements."

God listened patiently and then said, "Tell you what; if you can make a human being, like I made Adam, I'll leave.

The scientist agreed and bent down to grab a handful of dirt. That's when God said, "Wait a second! Go make your own dirt."

JUST IN CASE

If any of your students struggle with believing that science is biased, try using this explanation, which is based on the thoughts of C.S. Lewis.

Let's say the universe did begin by random accident, with no thought or purpose behind it. And let's say that life did begin by random accident, with no thought or purpose behind it. And let's say that humankind did evolve from something else by random accident, with no thought or purpose behind it. If this is true, then any human ideas would be, at their root, nothing more than accidental and purposeless randomness. So, any ideas the human mind could come up with about how the universe and life began would be purposeless, random, and accidental. And why would we believe an idea that is nothing more than random and accidental thoughts generated with no reason or purpose behind it?

- Is it more important to know how life began or why life began?
- If human life began by random accident, what does that say about what it means to be human? If human life was planned and created by a loving God, what does that say about what it means to be human?

Now What? (15 min.)

Option 1: Creation, Round Two

Send students back to the art supplies. This time ask them each to make an artistic representation of one part of God's creation, maybe even what they named earlier as the part of creation that makes them feel closest to God. Allow half of this allotted time to work, and the other half for those students who wish to share their works with the whole class. Praise all students' work. If you have time, ask some probing questions such as:

What that drew you to make a horse? What is it about a mountain that makes you think of God?

Option 2: Poems/Songs

Have each student pull five words from the word bag you prepared. Explain that they are to use these words to create either a poem or song lyrics about some aspect of nature/creation. Students may add as many other words as they wish to complete their poem/song, but must somehow include the ones they drew from the bag. Either have pads and pens available or allow students to use the art supplies to write their poems/songs. Allow half of this allotted time to work and the other half for students who wish to share works with the whole class.

Some suggested words can be found in the Leader Prep section of this lesson.

As a class, consider how you can share your students' artwork or poetry with the entire congregation.

Live It (15 min.)

Take your class outside the building and as far into nature as possible in the time available. Do this even if it means spending a few minutes in unpleasant weather. Have students form an outward-facing a circle. You stand in the middle. Ask students to spend one full minute looking, listening, smelling, tasting, and feeling every bit of creation they can, from the tiniest bugs to the sky above and everything in between. Explain that you will start a "circle" prayer and each student, in turn, is to thank God for one bit of creation he or she has noticed in that minute. You will then close with the following prayer.

Pray: *Thank you, God, for creating everything that is. Help us and others to see you in your work that is all around us every day. Today we especially thank you for…*

Resources used: *Confession of Faith*; dictonary.com; *God in the Dock*, by C.S. Lewis; getyourowndirt.com; scientificamerican.com; *The Interpreter's Bible*, Vol. 1.

© 2012 Discipleship Ministry Team of the Ministry Council of the Cumberland Presbyterian Church. All Rights Reserved.

JUST IN CASE

If any of your students asks why God speaks of God's self in the plural (1:26), explain that this is generally understood in one of three ways: 1) a discussion among the persons within the Holy Trinity, 2) a discussion between God and the heavenly host (angels), 3) use of the royal "we." The meaning of "in the image of God" (1:27) is also uncertain, but generally is seen as a reference to the spiritual part of humans not found in any other creature.

The Fall
by Andy McClung

Scripture: Genesis 3:1-13, 22-24

Theme: God created humankind to be in perfect relationship with him, with one another, and with the rest of creation. Human sin ruined perfection, and its effects are still felt today.

Resource List

- Bakery box or gift bag full of treats
- Pads of paper and pens for each student
- Internet and video playing capability
- Photocopies of "Prayer of Confession" handout, one for every two students

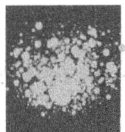

Leader Prep

- Arrange for one student to help you with the Get Started activity "Temptation" as detailed, if you use that option.
- Prepare and show the clip titled "A SIMPLE PLAN—HQ Trailer (1998)" or the one titled "A Simple Plan Trailer." The clip can be found at http://www.youtube.com/watch?v=hn81aL59Bjg.
- You'll need space for students to work privately.

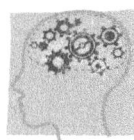

Leader Insight

Connecting to Your Students
Teens know about messing up. When he dumps her, she wonders what she did wrong. When she says no to going on a date, he assumes it's because he isn't funny enough.

Teens constantly stress over the potential of messing up. At school it's facing tests and grades. At work it's being under the scrutiny of a supervisor. At home it's being under the watchful eye of parents who are fearful of "typical teenage behavior," or feeling responsible for their parents' marital trouble. At play it's knowing their coach or teammates will point out any mistake that hurts the team. At church there may even be adults who like to point out when teens are

> **Leader Tip:**
> Some people mistakenly think the term original sin refers to sexual intercourse, perhaps because original sin is transmitted through procreation. This term, however, refers to a state of being rather than any particular act. In this lesson we're calling that state sinfulness. All humans are born sinful simply because they're human. That is why Jesus' conception had to be unique.

underdressed or too loud.

Yes, teens know about messing up. Some feel as if that's all they do. Maybe that's why teens so readily adopt our culture's fondness for not taking responsibility for our own actions.

Explaining the Bible

The temptation here is to try to decide if the story of Adam and Eve is exactly what happened, or if it's a metaphor to explain how humankind came to be alienated from God. Compelling arguments can be made for both sides of this debate, and exploring them is probably a good exercise for adults who need to clarify why they believe what they believe about this story, but we're unlikely to know the truth in this life. For youth (and adults), it seems far more important to spend our time, thought, and energy on what this story means to those of us who are trying to live lives pleasing to God today. There's room in Christianity for some to believe Genesis 3 is a literal account and for some to believe it is symbolic. It's most important to agree that God created humans to be in perfect community with God, one another, and the rest of creation; the first humans chose to disobey God (or sin), thereby disrupting that community; since then, all humans have chosen to sin; and that sin separates us from God. (See *Confession of Faith* 2.03–2.05.)

Several questions may come to mind when reading Genesis 3. One is the question of why every human being is affected by Adam's sin. Most folks can understand being held accountable for one's own sins, but it's not as easy to understand being held accountable for someone else's sin. The Hebrew understanding of the family was that the head of the family, the father, in their thinking, legally and socially represented the entire family. So, whatever Dad did affected the whole family. If Dad was a war hero, the whole family was praised. If Dad was caught stealing, the whole family suffered shame. (This cultural custom is quite evident in the New Testament when we read the phrase "… and his household.") Adam, being the "dad" of all humankind, broke God's one rule so his whole "family" suffered the consequences. Ever since, human beings have been born sinful. Jesus was the "second Adam." He suffered the consequence of sin, death, for the whole human "household," thus giving us the chance to regain that perfect relationship with God.

It may seem harsh to call babies sinful. But sinful and sinner are different things. Cumberland Presbyterians believe that any baby who dies—though sinful because he or she is a human being—has not sinned and, therefore, is saved by the grace of God. Children who survive infancy, though, sooner or later begin to sin when they choose to go against God's will.

Another question one might ask of this story is why God allowed temptation to be in the garden. This question will have to remain unanswered because humans cannot give a definitive answer. It made sense, though, for there to be something off-limits to the humans. If God gave them the freedom to choose their actions, then there had to be something to choose between.

Does this mean that God tempts us? According to James (1:13), God never tempts anyone. That only makes sense, because temptation is either evil or pretty close to it. Evil and God don't mix. God is good and cannot do anything evil. God cannot be tempted and God does not tempt us. Why would God, who is nothing but holy love, tempt anyone to sin? God did, however, give us the freedom to choose between good and evil. Because we are free to choose evil, we will always face temptation.

Another question is that of why God didn't just stop Adam and Eve from sinning. Surely God knew what they were doing. God could have stopped them easily. But again, that would have violated the free will God had given them. God didn't create humankind to be computer programs that only did exactly what they were told. Rather, God created thinking, feeling, imaginative beings with the ability to choose whether or not they do what is pleasing to their creator. An analogy might be the difference between a child playing with a stuffed animal and a real puppy. The stuffed animal is going to be perfectly behaved and "do" exactly what the child wishes. A real puppy may or may not do what the child wishes, but playing with it is much more fun, and more rewarding when it does what the child wants.

A final question we'll consider here is that of why God didn't just forgive the humans and allow them to continue in paradise. Maybe God did forgive them. But being forgiven does not mean escaping the consequences of one's actions. For example, a couple may forgive the drunk driver who killed their child, but that driver will still go to prison for a time.

Theological Underpinnings
At the heart of this lesson is one of the oldest theological con

Notes:

cepts around, and the favorite topic for many preachers: sin. *Sin* is both a state of being and an action. The state of sin, which we're calling sinfulness, is the condition in which a person is separated from God. We inherit this condition because we are human; as humans we will sin sooner or later, no question about it. Acts of sin are any choices we make that break God's law or go against God's will. Note, then, that we can sin both by doing something God does not want us to do (called a sin of commission) and also by not doing something God does want us to do (called a sin of omission). While sin is at the theological heart of this lesson, sin often begins with temptation. Temptation is the enticement to sin. This enticement may come from the world around us (whether from individuals, groups, or culture as a whole), from our own minds or bodies, or from the devil. While teens are hardly strangers to temptation, exactly what constitutes a sin (the deliberate act kind) is less clear to them. In fact, teens are often very interested in exactly how far they can move toward a sin before they've actually committed the sin. Defining sin, correctly, as "anything that goes against what God wants" helps that.

Both opening activity options will solidify the idea of temptation. The Bible study explores the result of giving in to temptation and the origins of humankind's sinfulness. The follow-up activities transition students' thinking from the temptation and sin of the first humans to their own temptations and sins. The closing activity stresses confession and forgiveness for when the failure to resist temptation.

Applying the Lesson to Your Own Life

With what temptation do you struggle the most? What sin do you find yourself confessing again and again? Is there some frequent behavior in your life about which you once felt guilty, but now do not? If so, what changed your heart?

What temptation have you become good at resisting, maybe even to the point that it is no longer a real temptation? What is your method for successfully resisting this temptation? Write it down and share it with others, especially those whom you suspect may be struggling with or giving in to this same temptation.

Does your church's worship service include a time for prayers of confession? This could mean either everyone praying the same prayer aloud, or praying silently, or both? If so, how seriously do you approach this portion of the service? If not, ask the worship planner(s) why such a prayer is not included in worship.

The Lesson

Get Started (12 min.)

Video Option: A Simple Plan

Show the YouTube video, "A Simple Plan."

Prepare and show the clip titled "A SIMPLE PLAN—HQ Trailer (1998)" or the one titled "A Simple Plan Trailer."

Discussion Questions:
- What do you think you would do if you and some friends found a bag full of cash?
- How might your actions be different if you found it by yourself?
- From this trailer, do you think things go well or poorly for the guys who find that money?
- At the end of the clip, Jacob (Billy Bob Thornton) says to his brother, "Hank, do you ever feel evil? I do." Is it evil to give in to temptation?

Transition: *Today we are exploring the first time humans faced temptation. They gave in. And it didn't go well for them afterwards. In fact, they messed up things for all humankind.*

Activity Option: Temptation

Place a bakery box, donut box, or gift bag prominently in the classroom. You know your students; choose whichever of these that would most tempt them to peek inside. If a bag from a particular store would be more tempting, use it instead. If you regularly have muffins or doughnuts in the classroom, make sure this box/bag is distinctly different. Have an actual treat inside, but be aware that you will have to withhold it from your students to make the point of the lesson.

As students arrive, say that the class is getting a special treat today. Don't directly indicate the box/bag. Then act as if you've left something in the car or you have to go speak to

Notes:

Notes:

Notes:

someone in another part of the building. (Don't lie! Really leave something you need in your car, or say something like, "There's something I need to do in the fellowship hall. I'll be back in a few minutes.") Leave the room. Stay out of the classroom until you think all students or most students, if you have persistent stragglers, have arrived and had a few minutes to notice the bag/box. Return to the classroom.

When you return, say something like: Our lesson today is about... Stop speaking and "notice" the box/bag. Take a closer look at it. Then ask: Did someone open this while I was gone?

For this exercise to work, someone must look in the box/bag. So, pre-arrange for one student to be your secret accomplice. This accomplice has four jobs:
1. While you are out of the room, to remind everyone that you said to leave the box/bag alone, but only if no one else says it.
2. To open the bag/box, but only if no one else does, and tell the others what's in it. If it's an edible treat, he or should take a bite and offer some to others.
3. To confess after you return and ask if anyone opened the box, but only after allowing other students a chance to indict him or her. You can work out a signal, such as sitting down, to indicate to your accomplice when it's time to confess.
4. To reveal that he or she is working with you, but only after the lesson is over. We don't want to promote dishonesty.

Transition: *Today we're exploring the first time humans faced temptation. They gave in. And it didn't go well for them afterwards. In fact, they messed up things for all humankind.*

Listen Up (25 min.)

Have someone read aloud Genesis 3:1-7.

Discussion Questions:
- Does the Bible mention what kind of fruit was on this tree? Why do you think the image of Adam and Eve eating an apple is so firmly lodged in our imaginations?
- Were you tempted to look in the bag/box earlier?

- Describe that temptation: what went through your mind? What do you think made you able/unable to resist that temptation?
- If one person whom you knew and trusted told you that eating a certain thing would kill you, and then a stranger told you eating that thing would be good for you, would you eat it? Why do you think Eve did? Why do you think Adam did?
- Lots of people teens know and trust tell them that certain behaviors are harmful, but when someone else comes along and says those things are fun, many teens believe them and do those things. Why do you think that is? What are some of these behaviors?
- If Adam and Eve had everything they needed, why would they want anything more? Do you have everything you need? If so, do you want more? If not, how much more do you need?
- What's so bad about wanting to be like God? Jesus was God incarnate, and aren't we supposed to try to be like him?

Allow answers for that last question. Then explain that God does want us to be like him in character (loving, compassionate, caring, forgiving, merciful, etc.) God wants us to become like God by following his plan, not by defying God's rules. The sin in this story wasn't the desire to be like God in character. The temptation the serpent offered was to be like God in power. The sin of the humans was trying to make themselves like God instead of allowing God to do it God's way.

Have someone read aloud Genesis 3:8-13.

Discussion Questions:
- Do you think God really didn't know where Adam and Eve were, or that God didn't know whether or not they'd eaten the forbidden fruit? Why do you think the story was written this way? Does God know when you've done something wrong?
- Adam and Eve immediately knew they'd done wrong. Do you usually know immediately when you've done something wrong? How do you feel after you've done something you know is wrong? Is it a good feeling? If not, how can you avoid feeling that way?
- Who does Adam blame for his sin? Who does Eve blame? Why do you think they didn't just own up to their actions and ask for forgiveness?
- Have you ever seen someone try to blame somebody else instead of owning up to his or her own sins or

Leader Tip:
In many churches, prayers of intercession are offered in Sunday school, youth group, and worship. These prayers might ask God's blessing on the sick, the bereaved, people who are suffering, and a host of other things. But how often do we pray for those who are tempted?

Notes:

mistakes? Have you ever done that?

Summarize Genesis 3:14-19 for your students. In this part God curses the serpent, tells the woman that because of her sin childbirth will be really painful, and tells the man that because of his sin he's going to have to work hard to have any food to eat.

Discussion Questions:
- Is God saying that woman's main role is to have babies while men should go out and work? Discuss how this impacts today's view of the role of men and women in society.
- God says these things as a result of human sin. So, if Adam and Eve hadn't sinned, would we have to work as hard as we do to survive?

Have someone read aloud Genesis 3:22-24.

Discussion Questions:
- Is it fair that all humans have to suffer because of the first humans' sin?
- If you'd been one of the first humans, would you have done any better than Adam and Eve?
- What are some examples from today of people suffering because of someone else's sin?

If students need a nudge on that last question, offer one of the following: a drunk driver kills someone and that person's family and friends suffer; a robber shoots and kills a store clerk who's a single mom and her kids go into foster care and later on welfare; people and businesses have been careless about the use of natural resources and now our waterways are so polluted that they are unsafe for swimming or fishing.

Now What? (15 min.)

Distribute pens and pads. Have students spread out for privacy. Allow students to choose between the two options below, or you may choose for them.

Option 1: Asking Forgiveness

Instruct students to spend this time writing a letter to all those who have suffered in any way because of something she or he did. Assure students that no one will see what they write, unless they choose to send the letter. Encourage students to focus on one act that affected a lot of people, but if this isn't feasible, students may write different letters to multiple persons.

Option 2: Resisting Temptation

Instruct students to write down the one temptation they have the hardest time resisting, using as few words as possible. Then instruct students to underline that temptation and map out a plan of resistance. The plan should have at least three steps.

For example: if the temptation is to drink alcohol, the plan might include 1) not going to parties or homes where people will be drinking; 2) to leave immediately when others start drinking; 3) to spend less time with friends who drink and more time with friends who don't; 4) pray for strength; 5) confess the temptation to a trusted friend or adult.

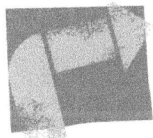

Live It (5 min.)

Have students come back together and hand out the "Prayer of Confession." You only need one copy for every two students. If necessary, explain how this works: everyone reads the prayer together, there will be time for students to pray silently, and then you will indicate when to continue by resuming the printed prayer.

Resources used: *Confession of Faith*; *The Interpreter's Bible*, Vol. 1; *Westminster Dictionary of Theological Terms*.

© 2012 Discipleship Ministry Team of the Ministry Council of the Cumberland Presbyterian Church. All Rights Reserved.

Notes:

PRAYER OF CONFESSION

Forgive us, God, for doing things you don't want us to do.

Forgive us, God, for not doing things you do want us to do.

Forgive us, God, for failing you with our thoughts, our words, our actions, and our inaction.

Forgive me, God, for...
(*a time of silence for personal prayers of confession*).

Hear our prayers, God. Accept our repentance. Strengthen us to resist temptation to these and all sins.

Lead us to seek out and make amends to those whom our sins have hurt. Lead us to forgive those whose sins have hurt us.

All this we pray in the name of Jesus Christ, who paid the price all of our sins, my sins, and the sins of all humankind.

Amen.

Cain and Able
by Nathan Wheeler

Scripture: Genesis 4:1-16

Theme: We are our "brother's keeper." God has chosen us not only to tend to the world, but to tend to one another. This lesson uses the story of Cain and Abel to talk about the importance of looking beyond yourself and seeing the needs of others.

Resource List

- A number of items around the room that students can use as an offering
- Four copies of the "Cain & Abel" script (Narrator, Eve, Cain & God)
- Bibles marked to Genesis 4:1-16 for each student
- You Tube Clip from the movie Year One
- For Option #1 in "Live It," have a computer ready so that students can read about the organizations, or secure information about the organizations and have it available in a form that you can share with each student
- Newsprint or Dry Erase board for option #2 in "Live It"

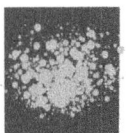

Leader Prep

- Instructions for each activity found in "Listen Up."
- Students to portray the four parts of the skit.
- Prepare to show the clip from the movie *Year One*. It is available at http://www.youtube.com/watch?v=LUmHo85M78Y.

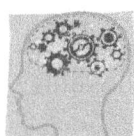

Leader Insight

Connecting to Your Students
There are a multitude of directions one can go when teaching a lesson on Cain and Abel. This lesson will focus on being your brother/sister's keeper. Many teenagers are wrapped up in web of self-gratification. Their choices so often revolve around what they desire and want, which leads to a false identity in Christ. As Christians our identity is one of selflessness not selfishness. With that in mind, the story of Cain and Abel is a good way of talking about selflessness and Christ's call to love others as he loves us (John 15:12).

Explaining the Bible
The first story after what is known as "the fall" continues in Genesis chapter 4 with the story of Cain and Abel. The stories of Genesis span hundreds of years, beginning with the creation of the world, everything in the world, and those who

Notes:

would care for the world. The compliers of Genesis focused heavily on human interaction with God. By the time of the events in Genesis 4, the first humans, Adam and Eve, have experienced creation, interaction, and condemnation in their relationship with God.

There is no time table given between the accounts of Adam and Eve being removed from Eden and the time Eve became pregnant with Cain and then Abel. However, scholars have pointed out the overwhelming similarities between Genesis 3 and Genesis 4. "Structurally, vv. 7-15 are similar to chap. 3, moving from temptation to sinful deed to divine interrogation and response to divine sentence and its mitigation to expulsion to the east...

Chapter 3 establishes a pattern that will be followed down through the generations. What happens in the garden in Chapter 3 and begins to manifest itself in disharmonious relationships of all sorts accompanies the history of humankind outside the garden in Chapter 4. The reality of sin continues and intensifies Cain's problematic relationship to God, to other people, to his own feelings and actions, and to the ground" (*The New Interpreter's Bible*, Vol. 1, page 372).

Looking at the story of Cain and Abel provides many avenues for discussion. Starting with the introduction to Cain and Abel, verse 2 provides us with knowledge of both Cain and Abel's vocation in life. Some scholars have pointed out that the hostility between Cain and Abel began long before they presented their offerings to God. From what information has been gathered about the ancient world, hostility between shepherds and farmers existed then and it continues in some countries to this day. The scripture doesn't necessarily hint that the hostility between the brothers began before the offering, but looking at God's response to Cain, it seems that maybe Cain already had a growing hostility toward Abel.

After Cain murdered Abel, God spoke with him. Some people have pointed out that God gave Cain an opportunity to be honest and confess his sin. Cain's response to God is one of the key moments in the Bible. Cain asked God, "Am I my brother's keeper?"

Cain's actions were violent not only toward Abel, but also to creation. God told Cain that his brother's blood cried from the ground and that the land was cursed because of his action. God's words proved to be too much for Cain, who pleaded with God to show mercy. God showed mercy

Notes:

The Lesson

Get Started (12 min.)

The Offering

Once your group gathers, explain that they will have a few minutes to choose one item from the room to use as an offering during your time together. Tell them that they will need to explain why they chose that item as there offering. Refrain from giving your group too many details regarding what the offering is for or to whom it will be offered. Chances are your students will connect offering with God, so they will most likely choose an item that will reflect that thought.

After a few minutes bring the students back together and ask each individual to present his or her offering along with the explanation of why she or he chose that specific item. If a student doesn't have a reason for having chosen that item, suggest he or she think about it or ask the student to select another item to use as an offering. Return to that student later so that she or he may share the reason for choosing that item.

After each student shares his or her offering, say something like the following: What we offer—whether it's money, our time, or some object—is as or more important than why and how we offer it.

Discussion Questions:
- When I say the word *offering*, what do you think of?
- Besides church, where do you give offerings?
- Why do you think that why and how we offer is more important than what we offer?

Say: *Today, we are going to explore the story of Cain and Abel. The crux of this story occurs when these two brothers decide to bring offerings to God. God accepted on brother's offering, but rejected the other's. This rejection caused a chain of reactions that included anger, sadness, deception, murder, punishment, and banishment.*

to Cain, but the movement away from Eden grew with every generation's failure to be its brother's keeper.

Theological Underpinnings

We must learn that how and why we offer things to God are equal to, if not more important than, what we offer. We all need to learn how to deal with our emotions appropriately. From time to time we all need to be reminded that we are our brother's keeper. We all are in need of God's mercy. With those truths firmly established, teach your students from a position that you have just as much to learn about these truths as they do. Teaching from a position of equality rather than superiority invites teacher and student into a unique position of discovery. This lesson ends with a chance for both you and your students to spend time together discussing what it means to be your brother/sister's keeper.

This lesson is an important one for all of us to learn, and we can approach the subject from a multitude of directions. This lesson offers two options for exploring the subject. Allow ample time to discuss one or both options provided in "Live It."

Applying the Lesson to Your Own Life

Have you ever been caught in a sibling rivalry, either your own or someone else's? if so, how did you handle the situation?

Have you ever tried to one-up someone in regards to your devotion to God or have you witnessed this among friends or church members? If so, erflect on how that affected you or the miistry in which you/they were invoved.

What does it mean to be your brother's/sister's keeper?

Spend time in prayer and reflection for this class.

Notes:

JUST IN CASE

Make sure that the students understand that anger is not always a bad emotion.

Sometimes our anger is justified, but choosing to do evil towards another out of anger is always wrong. Luckily we have a forgiving God who loves us, but that does not mean wrong doing will go unpunished.

Discussion Questions: (both options)
- Why do you think God accepted Abel's offering and not Cain's?
- Why do you think Cain killed his brother?
- What do you think God meant by saying, "your brother's blood is crying out to me from the ground"?

Now What? (15 min.)

Watch the clip from the movie *Year One*.

(The clip is 5:12 minutes. There is some language at the beginning of the clip that may be offensive, so preview the clip and decide whether or not it is appropriate for your group. To bypass the language, start the clip at :52 seconds.)

In the clip, it is assumed Cain and Abel were rivals. Some scholars believe that the true hostility between Cain and Abel began long before they gave their offerings to God.

"The story of Cain and Abel is regarded as expressing the age-old strife in the Near East between the desert nomads with their flocks and herds, and the settled cultivators" (*Who's Who in the Bible,* by Joan Comay and Ronald Brownrigg).

Offering

If your group doesn't collect an offering weekly, maybe you could decide as a group to collect a special offering and give it to a charity or cause that promotes being your brother's/sister's keeper.

Some organizations to consider include:
www.compassion.com (Compassion International exists as a Christian child advocacy ministry that releases children from spiritual, economic, social and physical poverty and enables them to become responsible, fulfilled Christian adults.)

www.onedayswages.com (One Day's Wages [ODW]) is a new grassroots movement of people, stories, and actions to alleviate extreme global poverty.)

Listen Up (25 min.)

Cain & Abel Dramatic Reading (Option #1)

Before reading the scripture, ask four different students to read the parts of narrator, Eve, Cain, and God. Hand out the script that contains the parts from Genesis 4:1-16.

The Story of Cain and Abel can be found at the end of the lesson.

Genesis 4:1-16: Lectio Divina (Option #2)

The term *Lectio Divina* (leck-tee-oh di-vee-nuh) means divine reading. It's an ancient practice of reading and listening to scripture that has been used for centuries. There are many methods of practicing Lectio Divina; the following one is a modified version.

Ask three students to open a Bible to Genesis 4:1-16. Suggest the other students get comfortable. After everyone is settled, ask the students to listen to the first person read Genesis 4:1-16. Explain that as that person reads they should listen for any words/phrases/or actions that stick out to them. Allow the first person to read. If pens/pencils and paper are available, encourage the students to jot down those words/phrases while they listen.

As the second person reads, ask students to listen for the dialog (the words of Eve and Cain). Once again have students note any words/phrases that stick out to them.

On the third and final reading ask the students to listen for God's words. Again suggest students write down words/phrases that stick out during this third reading. Ask each reader to read slowly so that everyone will be able to listen and with enough volume so that everyone can hear.

After the third reading, ask a few students to share what they wrote down during the three readings. Invite them to explain why they think those words/phrases stuck out to them.

Finish either Option #1 or Option #2 with these questions.

JUST IN CASE

There are many theories on why God rejected Cain's offering and accepted Abel's. Hebrews 11:4 says, "By faith Abel brought God a better offering than Cain did. By faith he was commended as righteous, when God spoke well of his offerings. And by faith Abel still speaks, even though he is dead."

Modern theologians have suggested that Cain's offering not was rejected because of what it was or wasn't, but because he brought an offering at all. The story never suggests that God asked either Cain or Abel to bring an offering. The crucial point is not the offering but what comes next. God warns Cain that, "sin is lurking at the door; its desire is for you, but you must master it."

Discussion Questions:
- When have you felt rejected? How did you feel? Did you get angry?
- When your emotions become overwhelming, like Cain's, how do you deal with them? At what point do you turn to God?
- What might have prevented Cain from killing Abel?

http://ministrycouncil.cumberland.org/secondmileprojects
(Second Mile Projects are opportunities for financial giving to selected needs. The projects are selected by Ministry Council staff based on needs presented by our fields of work.)

Live It (5 min.)

Am I my Brother's Keeper?

One of the most famous lines of scripture comes when God asks Cain where Abel is and Cain responds "I do not know; am I my brother's keeper?"

"'Keeping' is not something human beings do to one another in the OT; only God keeps human beings (see Num 6:24; Ps 121:3-8); hence God should know the answer to the question. In effect, if God does not know Abel's whereabouts, God has not been "keeping" him and should be blamed for his present situation. Cain seeks to relieve himself of any responsibility for Abel by focusing on God's task of 'keeping.'" (*New Interpreter's Bible*, Vol. 1, page 374)

Talk with your group about what it means to be your brother's keeper.

Discussion Question:
- How can we keep one another from being hurt?

Write down the responses on a piece of paper or a dry-erase board.

Close the lesson in prayer.

Resources used in creating this lesson: *The New Interpreter's Bible*, Vol. 1; *Jesus Wants To Save Christians*, by Rob Bell & Don Golden (specfically Chapter 1); *Talking About Genesis: A Resource Guide*, edited by Bill Moyers; *Who's Who in the Bible*, by Joan Comay and Ronald Brownrigg.

© 2012 Discipleship Ministry Team of the Ministry Council of the Cumberland Presbyterian Church. All Rights Reserved.

Notes:

Cain and Abel: A Dramatic Reading

Narrator: Now the man knew his wife Eve, and she conceived and bore Cain, saying,

Eve: I have produced a man with the help of the Lord.

Narrator: Next she bore his brother Abel. Now Abel was a keeper of sheep, and Cain a tiller of the ground. In the course of time Cain brought to the Lord an offering of the fruit of the ground, and Abel for his part brought of the firstlings of his flock, their fat portions. And the Lord had regard for Abel and his offering, but for Cain and his offering he had no regard. So Cain was very angry, and his countenance fell. The Lord said to Cain,

God: Why are you angry, and why has your countenance fallen? If you do well, will you not be accepted? And if you do not do well, sin is lurking at the door; its desire is for you, but you must master it.

Narrator: Cain said to his brother Abel,

Cain: Let us go out to the field.

Narrator: And when they were in the field, Cain rose up against his brother Abel and killed him. Then the Lord said to Cain,

God: Where is your brother Abel?

Narrator: He said,

Cain: I do not know; am I my brother's keeper?

Narrator: And the Lord said,

God: What have you done? Listen; your brother's blood is crying out to me from the ground! And now you are cursed from the ground, which has opened its mouth to receive your brother's blood from your hand. When you till the ground, it will no longer yield to you its strength; you will be a fugitive and a wanderer on the earth.

Narrator: Cain said to the Lord,

Cain: My punishment is greater than I can bear! Today you have driven me away from the soil, and I shall be hidden from your face; I shall be a fugitive and a wanderer on the earth, and anyone who meets me may kill me.

Narrator: Then the Lord said to him,

God: Not so! Whoever kills Cain will suffer a sevenfold vengeance.

Narrator: And the Lord put a mark on Cain, so that no one who came upon him would kill him. Then Cain went away from the presence of the Lord, and settled in the land of Nod, east of Eden.

The Flood
by Andy McClung

Scripture: Genesis 6:9–9:17

Theme: God gave creation another chance through one man—Noah.

Resource List

- Pens, markers, or crayons (no pencils)
- Single sheets of paper
- Pads of paper
- Watch/clock able to time minutes
- Animal crackers or other animal-themed prize
- The longest tape measure you can find
- A dozen cups, balls, orange cones, or something else that will stay put when placed on the ground
- Music player (laptop, iPod, MP3 player, CD player, speakers, etc.)
- Internet and video playing capability
- Rain or flood-themed music such as Jars of Clay's "Flood."

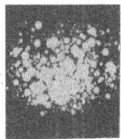

Leader Prep

- Instructions for each activity found in "Listen Up."
- You'll need a large space. Outdoors would be preferable.
- Prepare to show a YouTube video. If you have the ability to show your class a YouTube video, choose one of the clips of Bill Cosby telling the story of Noah's conversation with God about building the ark. There are several versions available (including one with Cosby's voice only, and the scenes being "acted out" by Lego figures); just choose one you like. Or, if you happen to posses the "Bill Cosby Is a Very Funny Fellow" tape, album, or CD, use it. (There are actually three different skits about Noah. For this class, try to find the one where Noah says, "Riiiiight" to God, which is found on YouTube at http://www.youtube.com/watch?v=so9o3_daDZw.

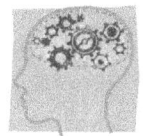

Leader Insight

Connecting to Your Students
Whether or not they grew up in the church, your students have probably heard Noah's story; it's one of the best known stories of the Bible. They may be old enough to wonder why it's touted as a children's story when it involves massive destruction and death. Children like cute animals, but teens are

OTHER FLOOD STORIES

The Sumerian story features an old man, Utanapishtim (oot-nuh-pish-tim), telling Gilgamesh (gil-guh-mesh), a king and hero, that the gods once sent a flood to swallow the earth because they were angry at humankind. One god warned Utanapishtim to build a boat to save himself, his family, and representatives of all living things. This story includes releasing doves and a raven, the boat landing on a mountain, and the rainbow.

The Egyptian story features Ra, the sun god. Fearful of humankind, Ra sent a goddess to kill everybody. So much blood was spilled it caused the Nile and ocean to flood. Ra changed his mind, tricked the rampaging goddess, and thus spared some humans.

There are three Greek legends about floods, and each has a Noah-like figure. In the oldest and most famous, Zeus planned to destroy humankind by flood. Deucalion (doo-key-lee-uhn), a king and demigod, received a warning from a god, built a chest, saved himself and his wife, and then repopulated the earth.

The Babylonian story also has three attempts by the gods to destroy the earth, the third by flood. One rebel god warned one human to build an ark for animals and his family.

The Chinese story has the gods ordering a sea monster to flood the earth for twenty-two years as punishment for human actions. A hero eventually dammed the waters.

ready for more.

In the story of Noah, there is the idea that something just isn't right with the world. Humankind has disappointed God once again. The world is not what it was supposed to be, so God starts over. Teens often have a sense that the world (or, at the very least, their world) is not quite right. Noah's story can affirm that. Additionally, teens can feel as if no one else in the world is like them, that they don't fit in anywhere. Probably not true, but it was for Noah, in whom such teens can find a kindred soul.

Explaining the Bible

Those who want to discredit the Bible are quick to say that there are lots of flood stories from ancient times, and the story of Noah is no different from the others. Those critics are correct—well, at least partially. Many ancient cultures did have a legend of a huge flood, and some of them included a lone person or family escaping the devastation by finding favor with the gods. Where these critics are wrong, though, is in saying that the story of Noah is no different than the others. Noah's story is different in that it has a very Hebrew twist to it. The focus is not on the flood itself, nor the faultless hero who defied the gods and survived the flood, but instead on a disappointed yet loving Creator who gave humankind another chance.

All these flood stories lead some to say that the story in Genesis is just one of many flood myths. Such an attitude, however, may primarily come from a prejudice against the Bible. An unprejudiced observer might look at all these stories from different cultures in different parts of the world, note their similarities, and conclude that some kind of great flood must really have happened for all these different cultures to have the same or at least similar story.

One can debate whether or not the flood really covered the whole planet. If not, though, it doesn't mean the Bible is lying. Stories from this time period were passed down verbally for many generations. If it seemed like the whole world was flooded to the people who survived the flood and passed along the story, then the biblical account is true to their experience. With that said, though, it's important to note that there is no scientific evidence that proves the flood didn't happen. In fact, there seems to be geological evidence in many parts of the world that supports the idea of a great flood. Some scientists, however, refute this evidence. Some Christians have come up with plausible theories about how the entire earth actually could be covered in water. One of these says that the "great deep" that "burst forth" in Genesis 7:11 was water contained under the crust of the earth, which may have caused the single continent to separate into several, and the "windows of the heavens" was a moisture envelope around the earth (see Genesis 1:7) which emptied all at once. Until then, the theory goes, the earth had never experienced rain, but the atmosphere was quite humid, which allowed plants to grow very large (geological evidence supports this) and people to live a long time. Who knows, maybe an asteroid punctured the moisture envelope and then hit the earth hard enough to squirt the underlying water upwards. The truth is quite muddy, as it seems most theories start out with a goal of proving or disproving the Bible.

Some preachers like to focus on the "wrath of God" part of the story: humankind had become so wicked, God decided to wipe us out and start over. It makes for a good pulpit-pounding sermon. But when we read the story, we find God more sad than angry.

Theological Underpinnings

God is gracious. Humankind did not deserve another chance, but God gave it anyway. The flood stories from most cultures involve angry gods and clever humans who outsmart them, some with the help of lesser gods. The Hebrew story is all about God, sad at humankind's sin, trying again by giving an undeserved second chance. Through Jesus Christ, God still gives humankind what we don't deserve: a second chance.

The first two "Get Started" activities simply get the students thinking about the many types of animals there are and what a task Noah had. The third option emphasize the flood more as God starting over than being wrathful. "Listen Up" puts students into the story of Noah, presumably deeper than they have previously experienced it. The "Now What?" and "Live" activities encourage students to be grateful to Noah for his faithfulness and to God for grace.

Applying the Lesson to Your Own Life

Do you think the flood happened exactly as the Bible says? If so, why? If not, what do you think was different, and why? Does it bother you that faith in the Bible isn't easy, sometimes?

How do you respond to all those other flood stories?

Recall a time when you really messed up and got a second chance. Who gave you that second chance? How did you feel

Leader Tip:

You don't need to share all of this information with your students; it's here mainly to highlight that it may be unwise to speculate about what happened so long ago based on those things with which we're familiar today.

Leader Tip:

No one knows exactly how long a "cubit" was in Noah's day, but later on it was about 18 inches (or, the length of an adult's arm from elbow to fingertips). If this was true in Noah's day, it means the ark was approximately 450 feet long, 75 feet wide, and 45 feet tall. It would have been able to carry the same amount of cargo as 569 railroad cattle cars. The word ark means chest or vessel.

Notes:

about him/her/them? Remember a time you gave a second chance to someone who'd really messed up. How'd it turn out?

What other Bible stories can you think of that we treat as being about a person or event, but they're really more about God than anything else? Do you treat your life as more about you and events in your life, or more about God?

The Lesson

Get Started (12 min.)

Have rain or flood-themed music playing as students arrive. Some possible music would include Jars of Clay's "Flood," Billy Joel's "River of Dreams," or Alison Kraus' "Down to the River to Pray." One report estimates there are over 5,000 songs about rain, so you probably already have a CD with one on it. If you have a "sounds of nature" CD, have the sound of rain playing throughout the lesson.

Option 1: Animal Charades

Divide the class into two teams and play a game of charades in which students try to get their teammates to say the name of an animal. Limit each round of acting and guessing to thirty seconds. There's no need to provide a list of animals for students to act out; let them choose. Award two points for correct answers and one point for "stolen" correct answers (that is, if Team A is wrong, Team B gets to guess.) Play for eight minutes or as long as it takes for each team to have an equal number of turns. Total up the scores, announce the winning team, and award them animal crackers or another prize.

Notes:

Option 2: Animal Lists

Divide the class into teams of three or four people and give each team a pad and a pen. Have each team choose one person to be the recorder. Explain that on your mark, each group is to list as many different animals as possible. Say "go" and watch the clock. Call for pens down at three minutes. Have the teams swap lists to count each other's animals and mark out repeats between the two lists. The team with the most animals listed wins. Award the animal crackers or other prize.

Option 3: Starting Over

Distribute drawing supplies (markers and crayons only, nothing erasable). Give each student a single sheet of paper, but let them know there is more if they need it. Place a recycle bin in the center of the room. Ask students either to draw a picture that's in some way related to rain, or write and decorate a poem that's somehow related to rain. Explain that this to be their best work, suitable for framing. Allow students to work until one or two mess up and wants to start over. You might want to form a secret agreement with one student to do this if no one else does by a certain point. When someone wants to start over, stop the activity and say: What do you do when something you're making isn't what you wanted? You start over. That's what God did with creation. (If the student didn't crumble up the artwork you do it now.) But instead of crumbling up a picture/poem, God washed away the part of creation that wasn't what he intended it to be.

Listen Up (20 min.)

It's awkward to read aloud three chapters of the Bible in class, so break the class into three smaller groups, even if that means one person to a group. Assign each group a section of the Noah story to read privately. Explain that they will give a summary of their section to the whole class—not quite the Twitter version, but, say, one minute or less. Allow a few minutes for reading, then bring the whole class together and have the small groups summarize the story in sequence.

Notes:

Notes:

Here is a suggested way to break up the story:
- Genesis 6:9 through 7:16
- Genesis 7:17 through 8:19
- Genesis 8:20 through 9:17

If you were able to find a space large enough in which to measure out the ark, take your class to it. Have three students measure off 450 feet in a straight line. Using the cups or balls, have them mark the starting point, the ending point, and a few spots along the way. Next, place two students at the marked starting point and have each measure off 37.5 feet by moving in opposite directions and at right angles to the 450 foot line. They should place a few cups to mark this line too. Your result should be a giant upside-down "T." Finally, have two students go to the other end of the 450 foot line and each measure 37.5 feet in the same manner. Your result will look like a capital "I." Have students place more cups, or move the ones already placed, to transform the "I" into a rectangle. Have students stand anywhere along the perimeter of the rectangle. You say (loudly): This is how big the ark probably was, and it was four stories tall.

If you don't have access to a large enough space, draw on an erasable board thirty cars bumper to bumper along one line to represent the length of the ark, and five cars to represent the width. If you have enough toy cars use them. Explain that if each of these cars is 15 feet (roughly the size of a mid-size sedan), this is how big the ark would be, compared to a car… and as tall as a four-story building.

Gather the students together in the middle of your ark outline or back in the classroom for discussion.

Ask for a volunteer from each scripture reading group. If no student offers an answer, specifically call on one of the students who summarized the corresponding portion of scripture earlier.

Discussion questions for Genesis 6:9 through 7:16:
- Some versions of the Bible use different names for the wood out of which God told Noah to build the ark (6:14). These differences occur because no one knows what the Hebrew word used there means. We don't know what kind of wood it was. Does it bother you that the Bible doesn't have all the answers you may want?
- Why did God single out Noah to save? (Hint at 6:9.)
- Have you ever been surrounded by people doing bad things?

- If so, did you join them? Why did you join them, or how'd you keep from joining them?
- Have you ever felt as if you're the only one around who's doing the right thing?
- Do you think people made fun of Noah for building such a big boat? When you're doing what you think God wants you to do, and that behavior goes against what everybody else is doing, do people make fun of you? If so, how do you react?
- How do you think Noah's family reacted to him building an ark? How would you react if your parents did something crazy, saying that God told them to do it?
- The Bible says "the earth was corrupt in God's sight," which could mean anything, but what's the only sinful behavior specifically mentioned? (Hint at 6:11.) Is the earth a violent place today? How do you think God feels about that?

Discussion questions for Genesis 7:17 through 8:19:
- When you think about all those people, animals, and plants dying, how do you picture God: happy, sad, indifferent, or something else?
- If we have the name of the mountain where the ark landed, why do think archeologists haven't found the ark?
- Suppose somebody did find the ark; would such "proof" make people who don't believe the Bible believe it?

There have been many attempts to locate the ark. Some have yielded interesting evidence, but most have come up empty-handed. One problem is assuming that the ark is on what we know today as Mt. Ararat in Turkey. Genesis 8:4 says the ark came to rest on the "mountains of Ararat," which sounds more like an area than a particular mountain. Besides, place names change over the years. There's really no way to know where the ark landed.

Discussion questions for Genesis 8:20 through 9:17:
- What was the first thing Noah did after getting all the animals off the ark? Is it significant? Why or why not?
- How is Noah like Adam? How is Noah like Jesus?
- The Bible never says Noah was sinless, just that he was righteous. What's the difference?
- Do you think God was more interested in destroying a bunch of people and animals, or in destroying sin and wickedness? What about today?

JUST IN CASE

If you have a particularly bright or curious student, he or she may ask about the weirdness mentioned in Genesis 6:1-4. While the subject of the Nephilim may be very interesting to the curious (especially those who like to wonder about UFOs and Sasquatch), it has no real benefit for Christian study. As Walter Brueggemann says, "The effort taken in understanding it will not be matched by gains."

JUST IN CASE

If you and your class are into movies, you may be interested in knowing that at the time of this writing (early spring, 2012), Paramount has announced it will be making a big-budget movie based on the story of Noah to be released on March 28, 2014. The title is to be Noah, and judging from the names attached to the film at this point—Russell Crowe, Darren Aronofsky, John Logan—it will be a good movie. Of course, announced movies don't always get made, and Hollywood has a strong track record of heavily changing source materials (in this case, the Bible). Other movies featuring or heavily alluding to the Noah story are The Bible: In the Beginning from 1966, and Evan Almighty from 2007, which would be good for a class viewing and discussion.

- There is no indication that Noah was a great leader, or rich, or influential in his day. Can God use ordinary people to do great things? How?
- In the Bible, names usually carry a lot of meaning. *Noah* means "comfort" or "rest." How is this an appropriate name for Noah?

Now What? (15 min.)

Option 1

Show one of the Bill Cosby—Noah videos.

If you have the ability to show your class a YouTube video, choose one of the clips of Bill Cosby telling the story of Noah's conversation with God about the ark.

Option 2

If you can do so without overly disturbing other classes, have your students divide into two or more teams and search the church building(s) for anything related to Noah, the ark, and the flood story. Send a pad and pen with each group so they can write down what they find. Encourage creativity in making the connections: the Noah's ark mural in the nursery counts, but so does an umbrella, and the numbers 40 or 150. Instruct students to be back in the classroom a few minutes before the end of class and share and compare their lists.

Discussion Questions:
- How is the story of Noah engrained in our everyday life?
- (If you watched the video) What surprised you about the video while listening to an adaptation of the story?
- (If you toured the building) What surprised you about the tour of the church building searching for Noah related items and references?

Live It (5 min.)

Gather your students together and pray the following or a similar prayer: *Thank you, God, for giving humankind another chance. Thank you, God, for Noah. Give us faith to believe without proof. Give us courage to follow your ways instead of the world's ways. Give us strength to ignore ridicule for doing what's right.*

Resources used: christianswers.com; flood-pictures.com; *Genesis*, by Walter Brueggemann; thewrap.com.

© 2012 Discipleship Ministry Team of the Ministry Council of the Cumberland Presbyterian Church. All Rights Reserved.

Notes:

The Tower of Babel
by Andy McClung

Scripture: Genesis 11:1-9

Theme: God has to deal with human arrogance once again.

Resource List

- Ten index cards for each student, and the teacher
- Unlined white paper
- A pen for each student
- Tape, or thumbtacks if you have a corkboard
- One-minute timer
- Building blocks, as many as you can get, or random items to use as building blocks
- Any kind of table

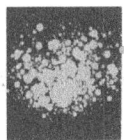

Leader Prep

- Prior to the lesson write or print words on sheets of unlined white paper. See "Get Started."

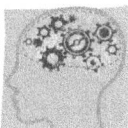

Leader Insight

Connecting to Your Students
Teens understand that there are many languages spoken throughout the world, and that each is equally important. Depending on your location, your students may hear or see more than one language used every day. They may have classmates who immigrated from another country. American schools are teaching foreign language classes earlier and earlier. Flipping through the cable TV menu reveals shows—even entire channels—that broadcast in a language besides English. All this is probably far less troubling to teens than to their parents and grandparents.

Traditionally, teens develop their own language as well. Slang is a way youth can distance themselves from adults, privately communicating with one another even if parents and teachers are nearby. This used to be primarily verbal, but texting has moved it into the printed word as well.

The awareness that shared language builds community,

Leader Tip:
For more on this subject, look for the FAITH OUT LOUD lesson: "How Did We Get the Bible, Anyway?"

Leader Tip:
The study of language helps determine what otherwise would be lost to history. In the Philippines the word for stone sounds like bah-toe. In Malaysia it's bah-too. In Fiji it's vah-too. In Samoa it's fah-too. In Madagascar stone sounds like vah-toe. This is significant because the language of Madagascar is very different from any language spoken in Africa, but quite similar to the languages spoken in this small cluster of other places thousands of miles away. So, presumably, at some point a group of people from the South Pacific traveled thousands of miles and settled in Madagascar off the coast of Africa.

coupled with the lack of prejudice against other languages, opens teens to be receptive to this lesson.

Explaining the Bible
The stories in Genesis 1:1–11:9 are called "pre-history" because they describe events occurring before writing was developed and thus were first preserved by word of mouth. These stories were not told and re-told in order to preserve an objective record of history such as one would find in a history textbook. Instead, they were told to help people make sense of things they couldn't understand, and/or to remember important events in the life of a people. That's not to say, however, that these stories are false; scripture remains the "infallible rule for faith and practice" (*Confession of Faith* 1.05). Maybe these events did happen exactly as recorded, or maybe some details were embellished and others diminished to emphasize the parts considered most important. The truth behind and within these stories, however, does not depend on their scientific or historical accuracy.

The Bible did not fall from heaven completely written. God inspired human writers to record certain things about God's relationship with humankind.

It seems that as humans grew to understand God better, the stories we told and the things we wrote about God became more accurate. For example: in Genesis 11:5-6 it seems as if God didn't know about the Tower of Babel until God "came down" and saw it, but by the time Psalm 139 was written, the psalmist understood that we can't go anywhere God can't see us.

After the flood, God promised never again to destroy everything (Genesis 8:21). Good thing, too, because humankind disobeyed God again. So God confused their language to encourage them to do what he had told them to do: spread out over the entire planet.

God could have forced people to go where he wanted, but that's not how God works. Foundational to Cumberland Presbyterian theology is that God does not control human actions, but allows us to choose our own actions...while hoping that we choose best...and helping us to know the best choice (*Confession of Faith* 2.00, 4.04, 6.01–6.05).

But instead, out of love for humankind, God maintained the integrity of human freedom and gave them a push by confusing the language. Even so, the humans could have stayed in one place and tried to work through the new language barrier. Instead, they chose to scatter. God never forces us to make the best choice, but does takes steps to insure we know 1) which choice is most pleasing to God, 2) that he wants us to make that choice, and 3) that help is offered for us to do so.

Critics of the Bible say the Babel story is made up, that any competent linguist or anthropologist can trace the development of all languages back to just a few root languages. They're partly right. Eighty-three percent of the world's population shares roots in just six different original languages. But that still means that in the past six distinctly different languages were being spoken. Plus, the remaining seventeen percent of the population uses languages from over 100 other language families.

Even harder for the critics to explain are the fundamental differences between, say, the language family that includes English and Spanish, and the language family that includes Japanese. (Imagine a monolingual American in Mexico looking for the airport. He sees a sign that says aeropuerto and can guess he's on the right path. That same traveler in Japan might walk right past a sign that says 空港.)

One who believes there is truth behind the Babel story, as it's recorded in Genesis, should easily be able to accept that the thousands of languages spoken today all come from a handful of original languages very different from one another.

We usually call this story the Tower of Babel, but the people were trying to build a city, too. This building project was very ambitious. Maybe this kind of brick-making was new. Babel may have been the first attempt at building a city; it's not clear exactly when the Babel event was supposed to have happened.

The word *Babel* may sound like the English *babble*, but that's just coincidence. Babel may have eventually become Babylon, the city that was the political and religious center for the Babylonian Empire we read about throughout the Bible. Babylon was in what's now known as Iraq. Babylon was known for its ziggurats: multi-leveled, pyramid-shaped buildings.

Whether Babel and Babylon were the same site is unknown. Some scholars say that in Hebrew *balal* means "to confuse," but others say that's an Aramaic word. A Hebrew word that sounds similar to Babylon, though, means "gate of God,"

Notes:

which may be a reference to the tower built to reach heaven.

Theological Underpinnings

After the flood, God told Noah and his family to "fill the earth" with people (Genesis 9:1). But here in Genesis 11 we find humankind trying to insure that they all stay in one place, that they aren't "scattered abroad upon the face of the whole earth" (11:4). Adam and Eve sinned by defying God's direct order, so they were cast out of paradise. Everybody except Noah sinned by creating and perpetuating a violent and wicked world, so God started over. And then some time later humankind again did exactly what God did not want them to. Banishment hadn't worked. Washing things away hadn't worked. So God tried something new to help humankind made better choices: God confused their one, shared language.

Centuries later, God gave humankind one last chance to regain that perfect relationship with him, creation, and one another, which was lost in the fall. This last attempt was by becoming human in the person of Jesus. Once Jesus had set into motion this final attempt, God reversed his action at Babel. At Pentecost (Acts 2), instead of language being confused and causing people to scatter, those who followed Jesus were able to understand one another regardless of their native languages, which drew people together.

The opening activity for this lesson highlights the differences among languages of the world, and the Bible study explains the Babel story as the origins of different languages. The responding and living activities emphasize the importance of using shared language to talk about community and God's love, and to help build community.

Applying the Lesson to Your Own Life

How do you feel when you see store signs in a language besides English in your town? in other towns? How do you react to the fact that 20% of the people in the United States speak a language other than English at home?

Can you speak anything besides your native language? If so, what led you to learn another language? If not, has it ever limited you? If you could easily learn another language, which one would you choose? Why?

How many times do you usually try something before giving up? Will God ever give up on humankind? At Babel, humankind disappointed God…again. Do you feel partly respon

Notes:

sible for what humankind, as a whole, does to disappoint God? When have you, personally, disappointed God? Did God give up on you?

When have you witnessed a language barrier push people apart? What about shared language drawing people together?

The Lesson

Get Started (12 min.)

Below are some words from other languages that have no corresponding word in English. Write each of the words on unlined white paper, one word per sheet. Write the word, its definition, and, the language from which it originates on an index card.

- *Cafune* (Portuguese) Tenderly running your fingers through someone's hair.
- *Zhaghzhagh* (Persian) The chattering of teeth from the cold.
- *Iktsuarpok* (Inuit) The feeling of anticipation when you're waiting for someone to arrive at your house and you keep checking to see if they are there.
- *Vybafnout* (Czech) To jump out and say boo.
- *Yuputka* (Ulwa, a tribal language of Central America) The sensation that something is crawling on your skin when there's nothing really there.
- *Pana Po'o* (Hawaiian) To scratch your head while trying to remember something.
- *Tartle* (Scottish) The hesitation you feel when introducing someone whose name you've forgotten.
- *Gumusservi* (Turkish) Moonlight shining on water.
- *Mencolek* (Indonesian) When you're behind someone and you reach around and tap them on the opposite shoulder to fool them.
- *Luftmensch* (Yiddish) The literal translation is "air person," but it means an impractical person or a dreamer, someone with no business sense.

Notes:
Linguists say Arabic, Cantonese, Mandarin, Japanese, and Korean are the most difficult languages for native English speakers to learn, with Japanese being the most difficult. An English word that's one of the hardest to translate into other languages is gobbledygook.

Notes:

Give each student ten index cards and a pen. You probably will not have time to play ten rounds.

Here's how each round works:
1. Place one of the words, printed on paper, on the board.
2. Each student is to develop a definition, making it as convincing as possible so others will think it's the real definition of the word. Students have one minute to write their definitions on their index cards. Feel free to shorten that time if it's too long.
3. Collect the index cards so that no one sees anyone else's answer, add the card with the real definition, shuffle the cards, and then read them aloud.
4. After hearing all the definitions, students vote on the one that sounds the most likely to be the real definition. Voting for one's own definition is not allowed.
5. Reveal the correct definition and the language from which the word comes. A student gets one point by voting for the correct definition and one point for each person who votes for his or her definition. Award five points to any student who writes the correct definition (or something close) on his or her index card. If this happens, do not read that card aloud; announce the extra points at the end of the round. Scoring can be on the honor system; each student can keep up with his or her own score.
6. Tally up the points and congratulate the winner.

Optional variations:
1) Have students work in pairs.
2) After each round, ask students to guess the language from which the word comes. Award two bonus points to the first person to guess correctly. Everyone gets one guess.
3) After each round, ask students to try pronouncing the word. Vote on the best pronunciation. Award an extra point to the winner.

Say: *There are over 6,000 languages spoken in the world today. Chinese is the most popular, spoken by about one and a half billion people in 31 different countries. Only a million more people speak Spanish than English (329 vs. 328 million), but English is spoken in more than twice as many countries (112 vs. 44). Arabic is the fourth most-spoken language: 221 million people in 57 different countries.* (Pause dramatically.) *Where did all these languages come from?*

Listen Up (20 min.)

Have someone read aloud Genesis 11:1-9.

Determine how many different languages you and your students can speak, even if it's just one word and even if no one knows what it means. Then determine how many additional languages you and your students can name, even if no one knows how to say anything in them. When you've exhausted the entire class' knowledge of world languages, announce how many languages the class named and then restate that there are between 6,000 and 7,000 languages spoken in the world today.

Discussion Questions:
- Is it weird to think that there are billions of people on this planet with whom we couldn't communicate?
- How might it help you to know a language beside your native one? How might it hurt you?
- Have you ever been in a place where you didn't speak the language? If so, what was that like?
- Imagine you've never been inside a church before, and then you show up at our church one Sunday morning. How might that experience compare to being in a place where you didn't speak the language?

Explain that God's scattering of the people wasn't exactly a punishment. It was God's way of helping them do what they were supposed to be doing.

- Has God ever done something like that to help you make the right decision? If so, tell us about it.

Explain that God wanted and still wants people unified in their worship, not unified just because they live close together and speak the same language.

- Do you think God is happy when a group of believers and seekers like this congregation put up a building, maybe with a big, tall steeple, and gather there...or would it make God happier for us to scatter abroad?

Explain that to build a city took advanced technology (baking bricks). Apparently when people figured out this new technology, they soon allowed it to draw them away from God.

Notes:

Notes:

- How do people today allow technology to draw them away from God? How do you allow technology to draw you away from God?
- What else do you allow to draw you away from God? (Don't let anyone answer this question aloud. Instead, use it as a transition into the following activity.)

Build Your Own Tower to Heaven

If you have a table, place some of the building blocks on it and the rest on the floor. If you're playing directly on the floor and it's carpeted, use a coffee table book, a piece of plywood, or something else that's flat and firm as the foundation for your building. Gather your students around the table and blocks.

A wide variety of building blocks are acceptable, or even preferable. So, raid the nursery, break out Jenga, toss in some Legos, and scrounge around behind the garage for bits of scrap lumber. If you can't find enough blocks, just use random items from around home or church: drink cans, food cans, boxes, books, etc.

Taking turns alphabetically by middle name, have each student state aloud something that people allow to draw them away from God. (That is, anything that takes up too much time, leads people into temptation, encourages people to make poor choices, etc.) As the student says this, he or she is to place a block on the table. After this, any student who has ever allowed the stated thing to draw him or her away from God also places a block on the table, building a tower. A more comfortable, but less effective, option would be to have students place a brick if they or someone they know has ever allowed the stated thing to draw them away from God.

Eventually, the tower will collapse. After it does, say something like: *When people tried to build the Tower of Babel, they were going against God's will. God did something to point them in the right direction. When we allow any of the things we've mentioned here to draw us away from God's will, God does something to point us in the right direction, too. It might not be as dramatic as confusing our language, but it's there. What are some things God places in our lives to help us do what he wants us to do?*

Allow answers without comment, but do share your own response.

Now What? (15 min.)

Explain that God reversed Babel at Pentecost, this time using language to bring people together instead of spreading them out. Then say: Let's join God in using language to bring people together for God's glory.

Have your class work together to come up with a new slang word, one with a spiritually uplifting or spiritually challenging message. An option would be to have them also come up with a simple physical act to go along with the slang word—something like a fist bump or high five, or using their fingers to flash gang signs. This will, however, take away from the emphasis on language. Only consider this option if your students are far more physical than verbal.

An example: GLU (pronounced the same as glue). It stands for God loves you or God loves us, but also contains a reference to glue, which bonds things together like we're bonded together in our love for God. This is only an example to get the group started.

Encourage students to use their new phrase frequently at church, at school, and in the community in the coming weeks. Encourage a student to post it on urbandictionary.com. Suggest your students make a video explaining the word (and the physical act, if any) and upload it to YouTube and GodTube. Ask the whole class to put it on FaceBook and Twitter. They could even try to put it on Wikipedia. Who knows, maybe it'll catch on and become the next big thing: T-shirts, wristbands, billboards, socks, a movie.

JUST IN CASE

If any of your students are into conspiracy theories or the ancient alien scene, be aware that the Tower of Babel figures prominently in some of those ideas. Theories include that the tower was made from crystal and was built to be a communication device, and that the tower was capable of verbally communicating with God or aliens. If these or similar ideas come up, gently say that those are questions best saved for another time.

Notes:

Live It (5 min.)

Arrange your students in a circle. Ask them to say the new slang word to each person in the room. If you have a particularly large group, have them say it to five people near them.

Close your lesson in prayer.

Resources used: "Balderdash," a board game by Mattel; census.gov; dictionary.com; ethnologue.com; *Genesis* (Interpretation Series), by Walter Brueggemann; mentalfloss.com; *The Interpreter's Bible*, Vol. 1; *The New Bible Dictionary*, "The Story of Human Language," a lecture by John McWhorter.

© 2012 Discipleship Ministry Team of the Ministry Council of the Cumberland Presbyterian Church. All Rights Reserved.

The Sacrifice: Issac
by Aaron Ferry

Scripture: Genesis 22:1-19

Theme: Living a life of sacrifice displays and expresses our devotion to God and others.

Resource List

- Newsprint
- Paper
- Pens/pencils
- Various art supplies as outlined in "Through Their Eyes" under "Listen Up."
- Music player (laptop, iPod, MP3 player, CD player, speakers, etc.)
- Internet and video capability
- Six copies of the handout "Abraham's Sacrifice"
- Music and lyrics to "All I Have," by Mat Kearney. Album: City of Black and White (Aware/Columbia, 2009)
- Recording of the song "Abraham's Offering," by Danielle Rose

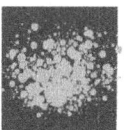

Leader Prep

- Pray for guidance for yourself and the young people prior to this session.
- Set-up the room in a way that will allow students to watch video clips.
- Prepare the music player (laptop, iPod, MP3 player, CD player, speakers, etc.) for use.
- Secure the "I Am Second" video clips from http://www.iamsecond.com. Prior to the lesson time, select the videos for Bethany Hamilton and Stephen Baldwin; have them cued and ready to play.
- Download music to "All I Have" by Mat Kearney and display the lyrics. They can be found at http://www.youtube.com/watch?v=ILO2hiHySBw.
- Cue the song "Abraham's Offering." It can be found at http://www.youtube.com/watch?v=SoJMdhDdN5c.

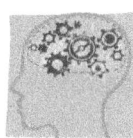

Leader Insight

Connecting to Your Students
Review the opening activities prior to the lesson and decide which one may work best for your group. Be sensitive to the issue at hand in "Last Minute Decision." Some of your students, or people who are close to them, may have recently experienced something similar and it may hit too close to home.

Notes:

As part of this lesson, you will discuss with the youth the idea of living a life of sacrifice. As Christians we are to give all that we have and all that we are to follow Christ. While this concept is difficult for every person, it may be an especially difficult task for the young people. Today's youth are involved in many different arenas: school, work, home, sports, band, arts, dance, church, etc. This generation has a full plate, and sometimes church and their spiritual life is not a top priority.

Explaining the Bible

People brought sacrifices to their gods from the earliest of times. A *sacrifice* was a "physical element" a worshiper brought as a way to express devotion and thanksgiving, but also to show repentance and seek forgiveness. The worship of gods and goddesses was a significant part of life in the ancient Near East. We see early in the book of Genesis where Cain and Abel brought offerings and sacrifices to the Lord, and we see Noah do the same after the great flood. These are just a few examples of where we see God's people offering up sacrifices to show their devotion, thanksgiving, and repentance to God.

Many different sacrifices and offerings were prevalent in the ancient Near East: burnt offerings, grain offerings, peace offerings, sin offerings, guilt offerings. Not until after the Exodus is there an organized system of sacrifice. When offering animals for sacrifice, the animal had to be without blemish and of a certain specimen. The only offering and sacrifice that did not require bloodshed was the grain offering; it came from the harvest of the land and was a recognition of God's blessing in the harvest. When reading the text, we learn that God was not asking Abraham to kill or murder his son Isaac, but that he was to place him on an altar as a burnt offering. In *Genesis: The New Interpreter's Bible: A Commentary in Twelve Volumes,* Vol. 1, Terence E. Fretheim says this act was to be one of faith with Abraham truly giving to God what Abraham loved (495).

In Genesis chapter 22, we see that Abraham has been a man of faith. But his faith hasn't always been so strong. Genesis 12 tells some of Abraham's non-exemplary behaviors and actions. When a famine hit the land, Abraham moved into Egypt. His wife, Sarai (whose name was later changed to Sarah), was a beautiful woman. Fearing that the Egyptian pharaoh would kill him in order to have Sarai, Abraham told her to say that she was his sister. Pharaoh did indeed claim Sarai, taking her into his household. However, God then sent plagues on the house of Pharaoh. When Pharaoh discovered the lie, he sent Abraham and his household away rather than killing them. Pharaoh knew that God had sent the plagues, and he feared God. In Genesis chapter 20, Abraham again tried to pass off Sarai as his sister, but God intervened in a dream to Abimelech in order to protect

Sarai and they are released (*Introduction to the Hebrew Bible* 93).

God had promised to be Abraham, but there were still times when Abraham's faith was shaky and wavering. However, in Genesis 22 we find Abraham listening, answering, and following God's command without much hesitation.

We encounter the life and experiences of Abraham in full swing; it is full of ups and downs. Abraham wonders who is going to be his heir and inherit all the promises God has made to him. Is it going to be Eliezer of Damascus, a slave born in his household (Genesis 15)? Or is it going to be Ishmael who was born to him by Hagar, Sarai's slave girl (Genesis 16)? After the birth of Isaac to Sarah, things finally seem to be clear, but then God told Abraham to offer up his son as a sacrifice. We, as the readers, know that this was a test, but Abraham did not. Fretheim says, "He [Abraham] has already learned to trust this God. He has no reason to distrust the God from whom this word comes, however harsh and frightening it may be" (*Genesis: The New Interpreter's Bible* 495). Fretheim goes on to mention that this act of offering up Isaac as a sacrifice was "an act of faith, a giving to God of what Abraham loves" (*Genesis: The New Interpreter's Bible* 495). Brueggemann points out that in this passage we see God as a tester and a provider, which can cause conflict for people of faith, especially when they expect God to provide, but not to test (*Genesis* 188, 192).

Theological Underpinnings

This lesson will explore the different images of God present in this story and how those images compare to our image(s) of God. This story of Abraham and Isaac reminds that God is a God of promises. In Genesis 12 God promised to be with Abraham and to make his family prosper and, despite Abraham's less-than-stellar actions, God remained faithful to that promise.

This story also reveals that God will provide. Abraham was faithful, trusting in God even when God asked him to offer his son Isaac as a sacrifice. Because of the relationship between God and Abraham, Abraham listened and trusted in

Notes:

Leader Tip:
If your group is large, divide it into two smaller groups and use Activity 1a and 1b, with each group participating in one activity. However, everyone will need to participate in Activity 2.

God to provide for the sacrifice.

Lastly, this story helps us to remember that God wants us to live a life of sacrifice and to give our very best to God, which can be very costly. Living in relationship with God and one another will eventually test our loyalty and faithfulness to God. As we grow with one another and with God, our trust levels are built up and our faithful responses to God and neighbor will eventually become second nature (*Genesis: The New Interpreter's Bible* 500).

Applying the Lesson to Your Own Life

As you read and prepare this lesson, remember that you are helping the students to explore what it means to live a life of sacrifice and to build a trusting relationship with God. Some of the same things that may be holding the students back may be true for you, too. As an adult, you may also be juggling many different things: home life, work life, dating, marriage, children, aging parents. What is hindering your relationship with God?

What is your image of God? What helps (or has helped) you develop trust in God and in your faith community?

The Lesson

Get Started (12 min.)

There are two activities for this opening section. Allow 5 minutes each for Activity 1 and Activity 2.

Activity 1 (choose one)
Option 1a: The Greatest Gift

Have your group break into smaller groups. Ask the students to think about the greatest gift they've ever received for Christmas, a birthday, or another special occasion. Allow time for them to share with their small group about this gift, giving as much information as possible about the gift, such as:

- Who gave you this gift?
- How old were you when you received it?
- If you had been wanting this gift, why?
- How much had you wanted this gift?
- Why was this the greatest gift you've ever received?

Once they are finished in their small groups, ask for a few volunteers to share with the larger group as part of the discussion time.

Discussion Questions:
- In your smaller group discussions, what were some of the greatest gifts you received? What made them such great gifts? What were some of the items that you would want to take with you if you had to evacuate your house? Why?
- Which of the items you said that you wanted to take with you were a special or important gift that you had received?
- What makes a gift, or one of those "special" possessions, so important and significant? Why and how do we place value on these items?
- When choosing a gift for someone, what criteria do you use?
- How many of you have ever received a gift that was totally not you or you thought it was not a "great" gift? How did you react? What did you do?
- What stories can you share about a gift you gave that did not go over so well?

Option 1b: Last Minute Decision

Have your group break into smaller groups. If you also chose to do "The Greatest Gift" activity, ask your students to get into different groups than before. Ask the students to imagine that they have to evacuate their home immediately because of an impending natural disaster. Authorities and rescue crews have given you 3 minutes to gather those items that are most important to you.

Discussion Question:
- What will you gather up to take with you to safety?

Allow time for the students to share with their group about the items they would take with them to safety and why these items are of importance to them. Once they are finished in their small groups, ask for a few volunteers to share with the larger group as part of the discussion time.

Leader Tip:
We understand that this may be a sensitive issue to some students and groups, so you may want to adapt the scenario; maybe you can use the idea that if you were stranded on a deserted island.

Notes:

Leader Tip:
If you do not have enough readers, combine the parts of Narrator 1 and Narrator 2, and God and Messenger.

Activity 2: What is "Sacrifice"?

You will need newsprint and markers for this activity. Write "What is sacrifice?" at the top of the newsprint or a dry erase board. All of your students need to participate in this activity, but if your group is large, you can divide them into smaller groups. Tell students to quickly brainstorm ideas, definitions, thoughts, images, and life examples (scripture-based or real-life stories) regarding the aforementioned question. They will spend a few minutes writing down as much information as possible on their ideas of "sacrifice."

- Allow time for groups to share their responses and look for similarities.
- See if your group can come up with a definition for *sacrifice* using the brainstorming that has just taken place.

Say something like: *When someone gives us a gift, and we hope when we offer gifts to others, there is a want and desire that there be some effort, thought, and feeling put into the process. We all want the best someone has to offer, and we should be willing to offer our best as well.*

The same held true when it came to offering sacrifices. A sacrifice was some "physical element" that a worshiper brought to God as a way to express devotion and thanksgiving, but also to show repentance and seek forgiveness. Early in Genesis Cain and Abel brought offerings and sacrifices to the Lord, and Noah did the same after the great flood. These are just a few examples of where we see God's people offering sacrifices to show their devotion, thanksgiving, and repentance toward God. Listen up as we explore the story of Abraham and Isaac.

Listen Up (20 min.)

Ask for volunteers to read the parts of "Abraham's Sacrifice." Give each reader a copy of the script.

After the students have read the script, use these question to help with the discussion.

Discussion Questions:
- What are your thoughts about this story of sacrifice?
- We hear from the scripture reading that God was testing Abraham. Why do you think Abraham trusted God and obeyed God's command to offer Isaac as a sacrifice?
- Imagine that you are Abraham. You and Sarah had waited a long time to have a child. Now that you have this long-awaited son, God is telling you offer him as a sacrifice. What is going through your head? What are you feeling?
- Abraham didn't even seem to question God about sacrificing Isaac. What does his response say about the relationship between Abraham and God? Do you feel you have that type of trusting relationship with God? Why or why not?
- Among those people with whom you have a relationship, whose decisions and requests do you trust without question? How long did it take to develop this type of relationship?
- We see and read that Isaac is the one who broke the silence with his father as they continued their journey. Do you feel Abraham's response was said to calm the nerves of his son, or an expression of his trust and faith in God?
- What images of God are present in this story? How does those images compare to your image(s) of God?

Through Their Eyes

Encourage students to use various art and writing supplies to look at the story from a creative angle. Whether through art, writing, journaling, poetry, etc., ask students to explore and enlarge their thoughts on this story of Abraham, Isaac, and sacrifice.

Say: *We are going to think about the different persons who were involved, directly or indirectly, in this story. We will explore and enlarge our thoughts and understanding of this story "Through Their Eyes." Select one character from the story, whether Abraham, Sarah, Issac, the ram, etc. and tell a portion of the story from that character's perspective. For example, even though we do not hear from or about Sarah in this story, you may chose to write a journal entry from Sarah after she finds out what happened. Or you may choose to draw a picture of the scene as if you were one of the servants standing off in the distance and you see Abraham tie up Isaac.*

Notes:

Allow time for your students to explore the story in creative ways. If time allows, have volunteers share their creative interpretations.

Discussion Questions:
- Why did you choose to explore the story in this way?
- Why did this particular artistic expression speak to you?
- How does this interpretation help you understand this story and your view of God?
- How do Abraham's actions, trust, and obedience toward God impact us as individuals or groups?

Now What? (15 min.)

Say: We hear Jesus say in the Gospel of Mark, "If any want to become my followers, let them deny themselves and take up their cross and follow me. For those who want to save their life will lose it, and those who lose their life for my sake, and for the sake of the gospel, will save it" (Mark 8:34-35, NRSV). Jesus was calling his disciples and those who were listening to join him on the journey. Jesus is calling us to let go of those things that are getting in the way of our relationship with God. Jesus is calling us to relinquish all things that are self promoting and aimed at taking care of ourselves. Jesus is calling us to live a life that is so meaningfully wrapped up in God that we will not want to let go of it. Let's explore this in the following activity.

Option 1: "All I Have" by Mat Kearney

Display the lyrics to "All I Have" by Mat Kearney so your group may follow along as they listen to the song.

Discussion Questions:
- What are your initial thoughts about this song and the artist's message? What do you feel he is trying to convey to his audience?
- What lyrics or phrases struck a chord with you? Why did they stand out or resonate with you?
- What connection, if any, do you see between the song and our scripture lesson today?

Notes:

Leader Tip:
If you are able to download and listen to the song, call attention to how the artist is trying to convey the message. If you are unable to do so, then ask for volunteers to take turns reading the lyrics aloud to the group. If your group is large enough, divide them into smaller groups and let each group deal with the whole song or just certain sections.

- Place yourself in the shoes of the songwriter. Imagine this song is a conversation between you and God. Where can you see and imagine God in this conversation? Where are you in this conversation? What do you feel is being expressed in those particular lines and/or stanzas?
- We hear the artist say, "All I have, all I have, all I have, well you know it's yours. Every breath, every step, every moment I'm looking for." What are those things in your lives that keep you from giving all of yourselves to God and others?
- On what things in your lives (school, work, athletics, extra-curricular activities) do you place more importance than your relationship with God and others?
- How might you rewrite this song to better express your longings and desires to live a life of sacrifice?

Option 2: "I Am Second"

"I Am Second" is a movement meant to inspire all kinds of people to live for God and for others. Actors. Athletes. Musicians. Business leaders. Drug addicts. Your next-door neighbor. People like you. The authentic stories on www.iamsecond.com provide insight into dealing with typical struggles of everyday living. These are stories that give hope to the lonely and the hurting, help from destructive lifestyles, and inspiration to the unfulfilled. You'll discover people who've tried to go it alone and have failed. Find the hope, peace, and fulfillment they found—be Second.

For this lesson, show the videos for Bethany Hamilton and Stephen Baldwin.

Discussion Questions:
- What are your initial thoughts and impressions about the videos we watched? What did you like or dislike about the video(s)? With what did you identify in these videos?
- How many of you are familiar with or know who Bethany Hamilton and Stephen Baldwin are?
- We hear from Bethany Hamilton's video that one of the paramedics whispered in her ear, "God will never leave you, nor forsake." How does this promise connect with our scripture lesson today? How does it resonate with your life?

Notes:

Notes:

- We hear from Stephen Baldwin that at one time there were many things in his life that were of greater importance than his relationship with God. What were some examples? On what things do you place more importance than your relationship with God and others?

Live It (5 min.)

Review the notes and brainstorming that came from the initial group discussion about *sacrifice*.

Close by playing the song: "Abraham's Offering," by Danielle Rose.

Closing Prayer: *God you are faithful and your love stands firm today as it did long ago. You have remained faithful to your people and have kept the covenant that you made with our ancestors. Give us open and understanding hearts, minds, and souls, to integrate what we have heard, read, and studied today. Move us to give everything we have to you so that others may see and respond to your love and your call on their life. Thank you for the guidance and teaching of Jesus, whom you sent to model for us the way to love the world. Help us to be a clear and true reflection of your love and your faithfulness so that we can make this world a better place. Amen.*

Resources Used: "Genesis" (*Interpretation: A Bible Commentary for Teaching and Preaching*), by Walter Brueggemann; *Genesis: The New Interpreter's Bible: A Commentary in Twelve Volumes*, Vol. 1, by Terence E. Fretheim; *Introduction to the Hebrew Bible*, by John J. Collins.

© 2012 Discipleship Ministry Team of the Ministry Council of the Cumberland Presbyterian Church. All Rights Reserved.

Abraham's Sacrifice
(Genesis 22:1-19)
An Adaptation of The Message, by Eugene Peterson

Narrator 1: After making and sealing his covenant with Abimelech, God tested Abraham, but Abraham didn't know this was a test. And God said…

God: Abraham! Abraham!

Abraham: Yeeessss??? I'm listening.

God: Take your son, your long-awaited son Isaac, and go to the land of Moriah and sacrifice him there. I will show the way.

Narrator 2: And so Abraham got up the next morning, packed the bags, gathered the wood and other supplies, and loaded up the donkey.

Narrator 1: Abraham got Isaac and a couple of his young servants and they were off on their journey, going to where God had directed him.

Narrator 2: As they drew closer to their destination, Abraham said to the servants…

Abraham: Stay here with the donkey. My son and I are going over there to worship God.

Narrator 1: And Abraham unloaded all the materials they needed for the sacrifice and gave them to Isaac to carry

Isaac: So, dad?

Abraham: Yes, my son.

Isaac: We have everything we need to offer a sacrifice, but we're missing the animal.

Abraham: Isaac, God will see to it that there's an animal for the burnt offering.

Narrator 1: They kept on walking together and finally arrived at the place where God had directed Abraham.

Narrator 2: And Abraham began building the altar. He laid out the wood and then tied up Isaac and placed him on the altar. As Abraham reached for his knife…

Messenger: Abraham! Abraham! Stop! Hold it right there.

Abraham: Yes! Yes! I'm listening.

Messenger: Stop! Don't go any farther. Do not lay a hand on your long-awaited son.

Narrator 1: What a relief. You could sense the desperation and relief coming from Abraham.

Messenger: Now I know. You obviously fear and have a great respect for God, you didn't even hesitate to place your son, your dear son, on the altar for me.

Narrator 2: Abraham's heart was pounding through his chest. He was breathing heavy with relief and then he looked up…

Narrator 1: Abraham looked up and he saw a ram caught by its horns in the thicket. Abraham took the ram and sacrificed it instead of his son as a burnt offering.

Narrator 2: And as Abraham was unbinding his son Isaac and preparing to pack things up, he heard from the Messenger again

Messenger: I swear to you, by God's sure and true word, that because you have done this and gone through this, because you didn't refuse me your dear, long-awaited son, that I'll bless you. You will be blessed way beyond measure. Your children will flourish and number the stars in the sky and the grains of sand on the beaches. All people on Earth will be blessed through your people because you were obedient to me.

Narrator 1: And Abraham called the place "The Lord will provide." That's where we get the saying today, "On the mount of the Lord it shall be provided."

Narrator 2: Then Abraham went back to his servants. They got their things together and returned to Beersheba, where they settled.

Sibling Rivalry
by Aaron Ferry

Scripture: Genesis 37

Theme: It is difficult for people to live in community with one another. It is so much easier to live in community with those who are similar to us because doing so is comfortable.

Resource List

- Newsprint
- Erasable board
- Markers
- Paper
- Pens/pencils
- Music player (laptop, iPod, MP3 player, CD player, speakers, etc.)
- Internet and video playing capability
- Copies of "Sibling Rivalry: Joseph's Solo" handout and "Sibling Rivalry, Discussion Questions"
- Video clip from Forrest Gump
- Song: "Beautiful," by Christina Aguilera

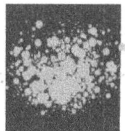

Leader Prep

- As you prepare, pray for guidance for yourself and the young people.
- Set up the room in a way that will allow students to watch video clips.
- Provide and set up equipment necessary to play music (laptop, iPod, MP3 player, CD player, speakers, etc.)
- "The Bully Pulpit" video clip from http://www.cnn.com/video. Select the video clip from October 4, 2010 and watch with your group. http://www.cnn.com/video/#/video/us/2010/10/03/am.costello.bully.pulpit.cnn.
- In order to watch these video clips, you will need Internet access and video capabilities in your meeting area. Make copies of the lesson handout "Sibling Rivalry" and "Sibling Rivalry, Discussion Questions."
- Download music to "Beautiful," by Christina Aguilera.

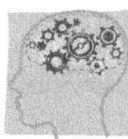

Leader Insight

Connecting to Your Students
In his book *Be the Change*, Zach Hunter says, "It's hard for teens to be in true community these days. We are all so different from one another, and we normally gravitate toward people who are like us. Being a teen is hard. It's hard to find your niche —and once you do, you want to protect it. So it's easy to get territorial and feel afraid to let in anyone new"

(41). It is easier for us to stay in our comfort zones, with what we know and what is familiar, than to engage and embrace those who are not like us or our group. It is easier for us to exclude and alienate those who are different from us than to offer acceptance and hospitality. The scriptures call us to be inclusive rather than exclusive.

Genesis is a book of beginnings, connections, interrelationships, family heritage, and all the messiness that is often connected with families. You and your students will explore the story of Joseph and his brothers as a way to discuss acceptance, welcome, and hospitality. Use these topics as a starting point to discuss bullying and violence among young people.

Explaining the Bible

The Book of Genesis has an important place at the beginning of the biblical canon because it is a book about beginnings—of creation and the numerous family units of Israel (*Genesis: The New Interpreter's Bible*, 321). "'Family narrative' emphasizes the family unit as central to these texts, and in a way that has no real parallel elsewhere in the Old Testament" (*Genesis: The New Interpreter's Bible* 324).

Genesis is a book about genealogies; it relates the connections, kinships, interrelationships, and family tree of Israel's people. Looking at families and their origins is one way to learn about the entire aspect of the family's heritage: the good, the bad, and the ugly. The Book of Genesis tells about the conflict, dispersion, and messiness of several generations; the story of Joseph is not exempt from these attributes. The story of Jacob's family, especially that of Joseph, is found under the umbrella of Genesis chapters 37 through 50 which, according to Fretheim, falls under the "Patriarchal History" of Genesis (*Genesis: The New Interpreter's Bible* 328).

The Genesis narratives often indicate the exclusion of some family members. In reading chapter 37, one would think the same would hold true for Joseph. It is easy to see the family conflicts and division amongst the brothers and relate them to the efforts of God's people across the generations who have tried to push out and exclude other children of God (*Genesis: The New Interpreter's Bible* 601).

Conflict, division, and exclusion arise out of this story of Joseph; these issues continue to plague humankind and are ones that society and the church need to address today. Several researchers and theologians attribute the conflict and division between Joseph and his brothers to Jacob's prefer ential treatment and favoritism of Joseph over his other sons. Jacob gave Joseph a beautiful cloak, which added to the conflict and division. It was a symbol of Jacob's favoritism toward Joseph (Difference and Dialogue: Reading the Joseph Story with Poor and Marginalized Communities in South Africa 164).

One of the difficulties and frustrations in reading and examining Genesis 37 is that there is no explicit reference or mention of God during the story. However, it was not uncommon for these theologians to bring God and God's grace into the story by talking about and discussing the entire story of Joseph instead of just Genesis 37. It is difficult not to look at this story as a whole because it is a witness to reconciliation and shows that God can work for good even through the worst scenarios Genesis: The New Interpreter's Bible 601). There is a difference in God working through turmoil and evil to bring about good, versus God orchestrating such events so that there will be an opportunity for God to do good in the end.

There are alternate points of view regarding the robe Jacob gave to Joseph. What Jacob didn't give the robe to Joseph as a sign of favoritism but because he saw something special in Joseph—saw him for who he really was? Brueggemann brings this idea further saying, "Jacob gives Joseph a special robe, a mark of regal status, and announces that this son is the wave of the future" (Genesis 300). So, if Jacob gave the robe as a sign of his awareness and acknowledgement of who Joseph is and what God is going to be able to do through him in the future, then there is reason to explore and question the brothers' reaction and treatment toward their brother. Joseph was just trying to be who God wanted and made him to be.

Theological Underpinnings

This lesson will explore the different images of God that are present in this story and how those images compare to our image(s) of God. As aforementioned, while there are no explicit and direct references to God in this text, there are several things that we can learn about God through this story. One can see God as a reconciler of relationships. It is also evident that God was present and faithful to God's people and kept the promises made to Jacob's ancestors. God doesn't play favorites or show preferential treatment; God remains faithful and true to the promises made with the community of faith.

Through this story we also see the prevalence of sin, how that

Notes:

Notes:

sin has caused division and conflict within the family, and recognize that God can work through sin and evil to bring about healing and restoration.

This text points to those who, pressed and pushed to the margins, are excluded and lose their voice and identity. But through this story, the reader sees God working in the human family, especially Joseph, to help him recognize God's purpose for his life. As followers of Christ, we are to give voice to and acknowledge the identity of those in the margins.

Applying the Lesson to Your Own Life
As you read and prepare this lesson, remember that you are helping the students to explore what it means to offer hospitality and to welcome the stranger; to live a life of inclusion versus exclusion. Some of the same things that may be holding the students back may be true for you, too. It may be difficult for you to step out of your comfort zone and interact with a group with which you are not familiar. It is much easier for us to stay in community with those who are like us and have the same interests.

Maybe you were excluded and left out; maybe others bullied and hazed you when you were a young person. Where was God in those times when you experienced isolation or exclusion? Who welcomed you and offered hospitality?

The Lesson

Get Started (12 min.)

Members Only

To begin this lesson, pass out paper and pencils or pens. Your students may do this as individuals or you can break them into small groups to complete this activity.

Say something like: *Think of groups within your school, community, church, etc. in which you participate or about which*

Leader Tip:
If your group is large enough, divide students into smaller groups to discuss and brainstorm.

you have some sort of knowledge, experience, or interaction.

As you compile your lists, think of how you are connected (or disconnected) with that particular group, what is the make up of the group(s), how does one become a member of the group, and how does the community-at-large perceive and describe the group (s).

Allow time for students to share and discuss with their group the discussion questions below, making sure to allow time for larger group discussion.

Discussion Questions:
- What are the different groups in your local context? What is their territory? Where are they? What do they do?
- How would you describe each group? How do you become a part of that group?
- What would cause someone to be removed or banned from a particular group?
- How easy is it for a person to become part of these different groups? How much interaction and collaboration exists between the groups?
- Is it possible to be part of multiple groups? How is doing so received by group members? How does this factor shape or impact your identity?

Say: *In his book* Be the Change, *Zach Hunter says, "It's hard for teens to be in true community these days. We are all so different from one another, and we normally gravitate toward people who are like us. Being a teen is hard. It's hard to find your niche —and once you do, you want to protect it. So it's easy to get territorial and feel afraid to let in anyone new" (41). It is easier for us to stay in our comfort zones, with what we know and what is familiar, than to engage and embrace those who are not like us or our group. It is easier for us to exclude and alienate those who are different from us than to offer acceptance and hospitality. The scriptures call us to be inclusive rather than exclusive.*

Genesis is a book of beginnings, connections, interrelationships, family heritage, and all the messiness that is often connected with families. We will explore the story of Joseph and his brothers as a way to discuss acceptance, welcome, and hospitality, and use this as a starting point to discuss bullying and violence among young people.

Notes:

Notes:

Listen Up (20 min.)

Sibling Rivalry

Distribute copies of "Sibling Rivalry: Joseph's Solo" and Sibling Rivalry, Discussion Questions" to your group. Make sure that there are a couple of Bibles handy in each group so that they can refer back to Genesis 37 during their discussion time. Choose a participant to read "Sibling Rivalry: Joseph's Solo" as a monologue to the group.

After reading the monologue, take a few moments to read Genesis 37. Once finished, if you are able, divide into smaller groups and allow time for discussion, leaving time for a large group report-back session.

Discussion Questions:
- What initial thoughts about Joseph and his relationship with his family do you have after reading the monologue and Genesis 37? What images does this story bring to mind?
- What dynamics are at play in this story? What are some of the difficulties of being part of a family with multiple siblings? How does/might this situation change with a blended family?
- How would you describe and interpret Jacob's role in this story? Did Jacob's love and affection toward Joseph play a role in the brother's plot to get rid of Joseph?
- What are your thoughts and understanding of Joseph? How would you describe him? In what ways can you relate to Joseph? It is apparent that the brothers did not like Joseph and that he annoyed them; do their feelings give them permission to treat him the way they did or to hate him?
- You will certainly encounter a "Joseph" sometime in your life. There are those people you have or will encounter who are different than you. They may have different gifts, talents, or abilities, or you may not agree with them or may find them annoying. How can you interact and respond to those individuals?
- What are your thoughts about Reuben's role in this story? While Reuben saved Joseph's life, the other brothers still sold him into slavery; they all conspired to deceive their father. While they did not kill him, they still got rid of Joseph. Is there a lesser of two evils here? While it was good that they did not kill Joseph, was it good for them to have sold him into slavery?

- How do you see this type of scenario played out in your daily life—at school, work, home, extra-curricular activities? Even though you may not participate in the actual bullying and hazing of an individual, is remaining silent good for you as a disciple of Jesus?

"I Know What Love Is"

For this activity, you will watch a short portion of the movie *Forrest Gump,* which starred Tom Hanks. Start the video at 0:12:12 and end at 0:17:22. Several times throughout the movie Forrest says, "I may not be a smart man, but I know what love is."

Show the clip from *Forrest Gump*.

Discussion Questions:
- Just prior to this video clip, Forrest says that his momma named him Forrest as a reminder that, "sometimes we all do things, that well, just don't make no sense." From the video clip, and potentially previous knowledge of the movie, what are some things that "just don't make no sense?"
- In what ways were Forrest, or others, excluded because they were different?
- Who accepted Forrest and showed him kindness? Why is it so difficult for us to offer this type of welcome and hospitality?
- Have you ever had to choose between standing up for someone or letting someone else take on that responsibility? What did you choose and why?
- What did Jenny, and others, risk when they defended Forrest? What are some real-life examples, either from personal experience or through media outlets, of someone having to choose between standing up for someone?

Notes:

Notes:

Now What? (15 min.)

Say: In the Gospel of Mark Jesus gave instruction and testimony to the greatest commandment: "The first is 'Hear, O Israel: the Lord our God, the Lord is one; you shall love the Lord your God with all your heart, and with all your soul, and with all your mind, and with all your strength.' The second is this, 'You shall love your neighbor as yourself.' There is no other commandment greater than these" (Mark 12:28-34). As aforementioned, the fictional character Forrest Gump says that he may not be a smart man, but he knows what love is. Jesus drives it home for us—the greatest commandment is to love God and others. Let's explore this in the following activity.

Option 1: "Beautiful," by Christina Aguilera

If possible, display the lyrics to "Beautiful," by Christina Aguilera so your group may follow along as you listen to the song. Play the song "Beautiful' by Christina Aguilera.

Discussion Questions:
- What do you think Christina is trying to convey to her audience? What lyrics or phrases struck a chord with you? Why?
- It appears that Christina is writing out of a sense and need to express encouragement and affirmation. What are your thoughts about the repetition of "words can't bring you down" throughout the entire song?
- What words really cut to the heart and cause damage? What are the "hot button" matters or issues that people demean in order to bring others down (i.e. family background, social status, demographic, race, ethnicity, sexuality, etc.)?
- How have you experienced negative words or actions that were meant to bring you or others down? What was your reaction? How did you handle that experience?
- What about times when you were the one who was dishing out the negativity? How was that experience for you initially? What about after you had time to think about the incident or see the effects?
- On the other hand, what words of love, acceptance, comfort, and affirmation can you share with one another? What words have you heard from family, friends, or

community that have been out of love and affirmation?
- How might you rewrite this song, or write your own song, to express your longing and desire to offering hospitality and acceptance?

Option 2: The Bully Pulpit

Say: *This video is about Kirk Smalley, the father of Ty Smalley. Ty, an 11-year-old victim of bullying and hazing, took his life because he could no longer stand the abuse.*

Watch *The Bully Pulpit*.

Discussion Questions:
- What are your initial thoughts and impressions about the video? What did you like or dislike about it?
- How would you define bullying? What are the characteristics of bullies and bullying?
- Where do you most often see bullying take place? Is there someone who intervenes or stands up for the victim? Who, if anyone, is the first to stand up for the victim? What risk is that person taking?
- As followers of Jesus, what can we do to stop bullying and stand up for those who are victims of this type of abuse?

Live It (5 min.)

As a group, write a prayer or covenant that you can use as a reminder to love your neighbor as yourself. May this prayer or covenant be a reminder of God's love and acceptance and a promise that your students will do their best to be a voice of love and acceptance in their schools, church, homes, and community. You may use this prayer, or covenant, as your closing prayer, or use the one below.

The following is an example of a litany/prayer:

One: God, you have placed us in your creation
Many: Because we are your children

Notes:

Leader Tip:
Encourage the group to think about and visit these other websites that deal with bullying and harassment.
- www.thebullyproject.com
- www.standforthesilent.org
- www.itgetsbetter.org

One:	You've given us one another
Many:	Because we are your children
One:	You've given us family, friends, acquaintances, and strangers
Many:	Because we are your children
One:	God, help us to learn
Many:	Because we are your children
One:	That where we come from doesn't matter
Many:	Because we are your children
One:	That how we look or speak doesn't matter
Many:	Because we are your children
One:	God, help us to celebrate our diversity
Many:	Because we are your children
One:	And bring us together so that we can worship and serve you
Many:	Because we are your children
All:	Amen.

Closing Prayer: *God, you are faithful, loving, and forgiving. Help us to be people who look deeper within our neighbor's being to see your masterpiece and your imprint. Help us, God, to take a risk and offer hospitality and love to those who are not like us and invite them into community. God, it is easier for us to turn and walk the other way instead of standing up for those who need our voice. So God, may we be a people who pray both for the victims and perpetrators of bullying and intolerance, and may we be a truer reflection of your love and grace. Thank you for the guidance and teaching of Jesus, whom you sent to model for us the way to love the world, so that we can make this world a better place. Amen.*

Resources Used: "Genesis" (*Interpretation: A Bible Commentary for Teaching and Preaching*), by Walter Brueggemann; *Genesis: The New Interpreter's Bible: A Commentary in Twelve Volumes*, Vol. 1, by Terence E. Fretheim; *Genesis: A Commentary*, by Bruce K. Waltke; "Difference and Dialogue: Reading the Joseph Story with Poor and Marginalized Communities in South Africa." Biblical Interpretation 2 (1994): 152-170, West, Gerald; *Be the Change*, by Zach Hunter.

© 2012 Discipleship Ministry Team of the Ministry Council of the Cumberland Presbyterian Church. All Rights Reserved.

Sibling Rivalry: Joseph's Solo
Based on Genesis 37 (NRSV)

My name is Joseph, and my father is Jacob. I have a large family—eleven brothers, only one of whom is younger than I am. Actually, nine of my brothers are stepbrothers because we didn't have the same mother. Can you imagine having such a large family? I had plenty of brothers with whom to hang out, play, roughhouse, and fight. But there came a time when my brothers were not too fond of me.

In fact, they hated me. They didn't have much to say to me that was very nice—they even called me names and made fun of me. And what sent it over the edge was my father's gift of a coat—a long robe.

My mom, Rachel, was my dad's favorite wife. He loved her very much. He was also married to her sister, Leah, as well as to the sister's maids, Bilhah and Zilpah. For some reason, my mom couldn't get pregnant, but Dad's other wives were giving him sons, which made her feel that much worse. Eventually, my mom and dad were able to have two sons: me and my younger brother, Benjamin. Because we were the sons of his favorite wife, Dad often treated us differently than our brothers.

The coat my dad gave me, well it was AWESOME—so colorful and beautiful! My brothers were very angry and jealous because of the coat. He loved my brothers and all, but I was the first son with his wife Rachel, so I was special.

I got myself into trouble with my brothers when I told Dad that they were not doing their job. He had trusted us to take care of the flock, and they just were not pulling their weight. That didn't go over too well. But then I really made them mad; I just kept digging the hole deeper and deeper. You see, I told them about some dreams I had had. In those dreams, my brothers and even my parents were bowing down to me. After hearing about the dreams, they really hated me, I mean REALLY hated me. My dad wasn't real sure what to think, but I could tell that he was taking in everything and thinking about it.

You see, I'm a dreamer. Not one of those daydreamers who stares off into left field imagining some outlandish fantasy. God gives me dreams and visions, so I have this special connection with the Creator. Sometimes I am not real sure what the dreams and visions mean, but I do what I can to pay attention and listen for God's voice and direction.

In order to find grass where our flocks could graze, we often had to take them to other places. My brothers had taken the flocks to Shechem, and my father sent me to check on them. When I reached Shechem, I found out that they had gone to Dothan. As I came close to my brothers, the recognized me because I was wearing my special coat. They decided to take advantage of the situation kill me! My brother Rueben convinced them not to do so—whew! Instead, they took away my coat and threw me into a deep pit. When my brothers pulled me out of the pit, it was to sell me to a caravan of foreigners. That's how I ended up in Egypt.

Sibling Rivalry: Joseph's Solo
Based on Genesis 37 (NRSV)

Discussion Questions

- What initial thoughts about Joseph and his relationship with his family do you have after reading the monologue and Genesis 37? What images does this story bring to mind?

- What dynamics are at play in this story? What are some of the difficulties of being part of a family with multiple siblings? How does/might this situation change with a blended family?

- How would you describe and interpret Jacob's role in this story? Did Jacob's love and affection toward Joseph play a role in the brother's plot to get rid of Joseph?

- What are your thoughts and understanding of Joseph? How would you describe him? In what ways can you relate to Joseph? It is apparent that the brothers did not like Joseph and that he annoyed them; do their feelings give them permission to treat him the way they did or to hate him?

- You will certainly encounter a "Joseph" sometime in your life. There are those people you have or will encounter who are different than you. They may have different gifts, talents, or abilities, or you may not agree with them or may find them annoying. How can you interact and respond to those individuals?

- What are your thoughts about Reuben's role in this story? While Reuben saved Joseph's life, the other brothers still sold him into slavery; they all conspired to deceive their father. While they did not kill him, they still got rid of Joseph. Is there a lesser of two evils here? While it was good that they did not kill Joseph, was it good for them to have sold him into slavery?

- How do you see this type of scenario played out in your daily life—at school, work, home, extra-curricular activities? Even though you may not participate in the actual bullying and hazing of an individual, is remaining silent good for you as a disciple of Jesus?

Revenge to Reconciliation
by Aaron Ferry

Scripture: Genesis 45:1-28

Theme: It is often easier for us to seek revenge than to forgive and reconcile with those who hurt and wrong us.

Resource List

- Newsprint
- Paper
- Pens/pencils
- Internet and video capability
- Joseph and his Brothers video clip http://www.claimthelife.com/ggt/ or purchase Good God Theatre: Act 1 Old Testament
- Copies of handout "Case Study: Skylar's Art"
- Basket or box
- "Temptation Island" handout copied and cut into strips for each group

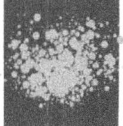

Leader Prep

- Pray for guidance for yourself and the young people prior to this session.
- Set up your area in a way that will allow students to watch video clips.
- Provide a way for the group to hear recorded music capability (laptop, iPod, MP3 player, CD player, speakers, etc.).
- Access the video clip "Joseph and his Brothers" from *Good God Theatre: Act 1 Old Testament* at http://www.claimthelife.com/ggt/. If you prefer to purchase *Good God Theatre: Act 1 Old Testament* to keep as a resource for your library, it is available online at www.amazon.com or www.cokesbury.com. If you are unable to show the video clip, at least let students listen to it.
- Make a copy the handout "Temptation Island" for each group. Cut each handout into strips.
- Make copies of the handout "Case Study: Skylar's Art."

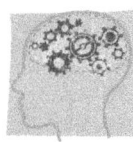

Leader Insight

Connecting to Your Students
Young people are faced with a myriad of decisions on a daily basis—both major and minor. They make decisions from what to wear, what to eat, what to do and where to career goals, college, relationships, and the list keeps growing and

Notes:

growing. Being a teen is hard. It's hard to find your niche. But we have to help them find their place and help them be prepared to make decisions on their own.

As you and your students explore this particular story of Joseph's life, you will be looking at the temptations Joseph faced, especially in regard to power and revenge, but how in the long run he was able to move in the direction of forgiveness, reconciliation, and healing.

Explaining the Bible

The Book of Genesis has an important place at the beginning of the biblical canon because it is a book about beginnings—of creation and the numerous family units of Israel (*Genesis: The New Interpreter's Bible*, 321). "'Family narrative' emphasizes the family unit as central to these texts, and in a way that has no real parallel elsewhere in the Old Testament" (*Genesis: The New Interpreter's Bible* 324).

Genesis is a book about genealogies; it relates the connections, kinships, interrelationships, and family tree of Israel's people. Looking at families and their origins is one way to learn about the entire aspect of the family's heritage: the good, the bad, and the ugly. The Book of Genesis tells about the conflict, dispersion, and messiness of several generations; the story of Joseph is not exempt from these attributes. The story of Jacob's family, especially that of Joseph, is found under the umbrella of Genesis chapters 37 through 50 which, according to Fretheim, falls under the "Patriarchal History" of Genesis (*Genesis: The New Interpreter's Bible* 328).

The Genesis narratives often indicate the exclusion of some family members. In reading chapter 37, one would think the same would hold true for Joseph. It is easy to see the family conflicts and division amongst the brothers and relate them to the efforts of God's people across the generations who have tried to push out and exclude other children of God (*Genesis: The New Interpreter's Bible* 601).

Conflict, division, and exclusion are issues that arise out of this story of Joseph, not unlike issues that need to be addressed today by society and the church. It is important to look at the story of Joseph in whole in order to see that this story is one of witness to reconciliation and God's power to work through the worst scenarios in order for good (*Genesis: The New Interpreter's Bible* 601). There is a difference in God working through turmoil and evil to bring about good, versus God orchestrating such events so that there will be an opportunity for God to do good in the end.

Temptation and revenge, forgiveness and reconciliation are all things with which we, as Christians, wrestle and struggle. The same holds true in the story of Joseph as found toward the end of Genesis. The reader learns early on in the Joseph story that his brothers hated him because their father's favoritism. To make matters worse, Joseph was a dreamer who revealed his dreams to his brothers, making it evident that he thought that one day his family would bow down to him. While the brothers were away tending to the flocks, they conspired to kill Joseph. Reuben, the oldest of the twelve brothers, intervened and suggested throwing him into a pit from which he later planned to rescue him. Later, the brothers sold him to a group of traveling merchants attempted to cover it up by telling Jacob that they had found his blood-stained coat and that he had undoubtedly been killed by a wild animal.

When the merchant caravan arrived in Egypt, they sold Joseph as a slave. Potiphar, his new master, was one of Pharaoh's officers. Things were going pretty well until Potiphar's wife decided to pursue the handsome young Joseph. Despite her relentless pursuit and temptings, Joseph continued to resist her seduction. His resistance landed him in jail because Potiphar's wife lied and said he was trying to seduce her.

Dreams continued to have an important role in Joseph's life even while he was in prison. When two of his fellow prisoners had confusing dreams, God enabled Joseph to interpret their dreams, which eventually led to Joseph being called to interpret Pharaoh's dreams. Through this turn of events, Joseph rose to and fell from a position of power not once, but twice (*Introduction to the Hebrew Bible* 102). From Joseph and the dream sequences we learn about his reliance upon and connection with God. Joseph made it well known throughout the scriptures that God was revealing things to him through dreams—his own and those of others—thus connecting Pharaoh and God in a direct relationship

Joseph rose to power because of his ability to interpret the pharaoh's dreams and was placed in a position of authority over all of Egypt. During this time, he implemented his plan to store grain for the people of Egypt because a famine would hit the area.

The famine was not limited to Egypt; Jacob sent his sons to Egypt to buy grain. Joseph was overseeing the purchase of

Notes:

grain and recognized his brothers, but they did not recognize him. Joseph's earlier dream came to fruition as his brothers bowed before him. Joseph tested his brothers to see if they had changed. When they "passed" his tests, Joseph could contain himself no longer and revealed his identity. Instead of seeking revenge and holding a grudge, Joseph sought healing and reconciliation The famine resultrf in the reunion of Joseph and his brothers. (*Introduction to the Hebrew Bible* 102).

Upon their return to Egypt, the brothers were received by the steward of the house of Joseph. When they were brought to Joseph's house, they became afraid because of the returned money in their grain sacks. They thought that the missed transaction would somehow be used against them as way to arrest them as slaves and confiscate their possessions. So they immediately informed the steward of what had transpired to get a feel of the situation. But, the steward put them at ease telling them not to worry about the money, and then he brought out their brother Simeon. They all went into the house of Joseph and were received with hospitality. They still didn't know it was their brother Joseph. When Joseph appeared, they gave him gifts from their father. Joseph saw and inquired of Benjamin and was overcome by emotion but did not show it to them. He retreated to a separate room and wept. When he gained control of himself, he returned and brought out the feast. At that time, Egyptians did not allow Hebrews to eat with them at the same table, because that was considered improper. So when the viceroy brought food over to the table of the sons of Jacob, they were astonished. Joseph showed great kindness to them. He treated them nobly. In a day of famine, it was enough to be fed, but they were given a feast. Their cares and fears were now put to rest, and they ate their bread with joy, deciding they were on good terms with the lord of the land. If God accepts our works, our presence, we have reason to be cheerful.

That night, Joseph ordered his steward to load the brother's donkeys with food and all their money. The money they brought was double what they had from the first trip. Secretly, Joseph also ordered that his silver cup be put in Benjamin's sack. Joseph was trying to discern how his brothers felt towards Benjamin. Had they envied and hated the other son of Rachel as they had hated him? If they still needed more of the love of their father Jacob, they would now have to show their true colors. When the cup was found with Benjamin, they would have a reason to leave him to be a slave. The following morning the brothers began their journey back to

Canaan. At Joseph's command, the steward apprehended them and interrogated them about the silver cup. The steward found the cup in Benjamin's sack because he had planted it there the night before. This caused a stir among the brothers. However, they agreed to be brought back to Egypt. When the viceroy (Joseph) confronted them about the silver cup, he demanded that the one who possessed the cup in his bag be his slave. In response, Judah pleaded with the viceroy that Benjamin be allowed to return to his father, and he himself could be kept in Benjamin's place as slave.

Joseph let Judah go on, and heard all he had to say. He found his brothers humbled by their sins, mindful of Joseph, for Judah had mentioned him twice in his speech. They were now respectful of their father and very protective of their brother Benjamin. Now they were ready to know who Joseph really was. Joseph ordered all his attendants to leave the room. Joseph shed tears and threw off the act he had been performing. "I am Joseph, your brother." This humbled them even more because they had sinned against him, but encouraged them to hope for kind treatment. Joseph showed them that whatever they thought to do against him, God had brought good out of it. Joseph promised to take care of their father and all the family. After Joseph had embraced Benjamin, he hugged them all and his brothers talked freely about all that had happened in his father's house since he'd been gone.

To hear that Joseph was alive was good news; almost too good to be true. When Jacob heard it, he fainted, for he didn't believe it. Jacob was finally convinced of the truth. Jacob was old, and did not expect to live long. He said he wanted his eyes to be revived with the sight of Joseph before he died, and then he would need nothing else to make him happy.

Theological Underpinnings
There is definitely evidence throughout this story of Joseph and his brothers that there is a wrestling match between good and evil, but we are able to see how God can bring good out of what was initially intended to be evil. Through this story of Joseph, we see God working in the human family, especially through Joseph, to provide healing and reconciliation.

In this lesson, students will explore temptation, revenge, forgiveness, and reconciliation through the story of Joseph and his famiy. They will consider how the situation could have ended very differently, but through God's guidance and

Notes:

Notes:

forgiveness gave way to living into the love and faithfulness of God.

Applying the Lesson to Your Own Life
As you are reading and preparing this lesson, remember that you are helping the students to explore forgiveness and reconciliation. More times than not, we want to seek revenge or to one up the other person rather than forgive and reconcile.

Where was God in those times when you experienced pain and wanted to get even? To whom do you find it difficult to offer forgiveness? Are there people in your life whom you haven't forgiven? Identify those people whom you have hurt or wronged who have offered you forgiveness.

The Lesson

Get Started (12 min.)

Temptation Island

Divide the students into two groups.

Give each group a basket, box, or something from which they can draw slips of paper. Each slip of paper lists a different temptation over which the individual will deliberate. The group to which the individual belongs is to give reasons as to why he or she shouldn't give in to the particular temptation. The other group will try to affirm the temptation and give reasons why it is OK to give into temptation.

Have each team take a few turns.

Allow time for students to share and discuss the questions below within their group or with the larger group.

Discussion Questions:
- Which temptations are especially tempting and inviting? Why?

- What are some other possible responses to the temptations we heard?
- How might we guard ourselves from these, and other, temptations?
- What are some of the most difficult and powerful temptations today's young people face?
- If someone asked you for advice about how to deal with temptations, what would you tell them?
- How might God help us when we are faced with temptations that are really hard to ignore?

Say: *Temptation and revenge, forgiveness and reconciliation are all things with which we, as Christians, wrestle and struggle. The same holds true in the story of Joseph as found toward the end of Genesis.*

The caravan to which Joseph's brothers sold him, took him to Egypt where he was sold as a slave. His new master, Potiphar, was one of the pharaoh's officers. Joseph was a very handsome man, and he attracted the attention of Potiphar's wife. She pursued and tempted Joseph, but he resisted over and over. She eventually falsely accused Joseph of pursuing her, which caused him to be thrown into prison.

While in prison, Joseph continued to have dreams. He also interpreted the dreams of some prisoners. When the pharaoh learned of his ability, he summoned Joseph to interpret two of his own dreams that were confusing and troubling. Joseph found favor with Pharaoh, who made him second-in-command of all Egypt.

Finally, we learn that Joseph's family in Canaan was desperate for food. Having heard that there was food in Egypt, they went to Egypt to buy food. Joseph recognized them and began to negotiate with them, making them prove that they were not spies. And now, here's the rest of the story.

Listen Up (20 min.)

Ask one or more persons to read Genesis 45:1-28.

Joseph and his Bothers

After reading this passage of scripture, watch the video clip

Notes:

from *Good God Theatre: Act 1 Old Testament* "Joseph and his Brothers."

Discussion Questions:
- What are your initial thoughts and reflections about this passage of scripture? What words or images come to mind?
- How did viewing (or listening to) the video help you to see this story in a different light? Maybe this video clip was not helpful to you. If so, why?
- What temptations did Joseph face in dealing with his brothers? What temptations did Joseph face after being sold into slavery?
- We see in the scripture reading, and from the video, that Joseph had suffered much pain. However, we learn that Joseph felt and saw God's hand at work in his life. Where do we see that in this story?
- Where do we see the hand of God at work in our lives, even though we may be going through difficult times?

Now What? (15 min.)

Throughout Joseph's life, we see a difficult and challenging process of making the right decisions. There were many opportunities for him to seek revenge, but we see movement toward reconciliation. As a response to this story, there are two options to further explore this passage of scripture and its message.

Option #1: Alternative Ending

Say: Have you ever thought, "What if the story happened or ended this way"? Here's your chance to explore that thought process. You may work individually or in small groups. Think creatively about an alternative ending to this familiar Bible story.

Allow time to share the alternate ending of the story of Joseph.

Option #2: "Case Study: Skylar's Art"

Work in small groups to read and discuss the handout "Case Study: Skylar's Art." Give the group time to read through the case study and then discuss the questions in their small group. Allow time for a report back and discussion with the larger group.

Option #3: Prayer Partners

Write down any temptation(s) that you are facing right now that are difficult for you to handle. Next to each temptation, write a strategy that you could use to help you overcome this temptation.

For example: Find a prayer partner you trust and in whom you can confide who will hold you accountable.

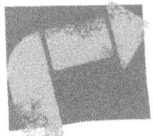

Live It (5 min.)

Have students make a list of those individuals to whom they look up because they are good examples and role models of how to offer forgiveness and reconciliation.

This list could include people who are currently in their lives (parent, teacher, friend) or people of history (Martin Luther King, Jr., or Ghandi). Take time to speak with or research their lives and see what it took for them to be able to offer forgiveness and work for reconciliation.

Closing Prayer: *God, you sent your son as an example of how to live life in a new way. Help us to quit looking over our shoulders at those things people have done to harm us. Help us to quit harboring negative feelings toward those who wrong us. Move us forward to a life of forgiveness and reconciliation. We often mess up ourselves, but you forgive us. Help us to forgive ourselves and to live into your love and faithfulness. Stay with us, God, and guide us on this long journey because we need your guidance and direction. Amen.*

Resources Used: "Genesis" (*Interpretation: A Bible Commentary for Teaching and Preaching*), by Walter Brueggemann; *Genesis: The New Interpreter's Bible: A Commentary in Twelve Volumes*, Vol. 1, by Terence E. Fretheim; *Introduction to the Hebrew Bible*, by John J. Collins; *The Book of Uncommon Prayer*, by Steven Case.

© 2012 Discipleship Ministry Team of the Ministry Council of the Cumberland Presbyterian Church. All Rights Reserved.

Notes:

Temptation Island

You want to break up with your boyfriend/girlfriend, so you're acting really mean toward him or her. Is this OK?

Someone wants to sell you a brand new Mac Book at a really discounted price. You suspect that it is stolen merchandise. Is it OK to purchase?

You would like to fight the school bully who has been picking on you and your friends. Why or why not?

You finally have the money to go to a concert by your favorite group, but the tickets are sold out. You have found a way to get in for free through an unlocked back door. What do you do?

Calculus is your toughest class this semester, and you need to make an A on the final exam in order to pass the class. Someone has offered to help you cheat so that you can make an A. What do you do?

You find a wallet that is filled with a lot of cash. You are in need of some extra money. Is it ok to take just a couple of twenties?

You don't feel like going to work today, so you decide to call in sick. What's wrong with that?

A young man/woman who is very popular and attractive at your school has asked if you'd like to go out on a date and hook-up. You, however, have been dating your boyfriend/girlfriend for over a year now. This other person says it's just for fun and that he or she will never say anything. What's the problem with having a little fun?

Case Study: Skylar's Art

Skylar is a very creative young woman who loves all forms of art. She has a gift and an artistic eye, and she uses various art mediums to display her talents. Skylar is a senior and is taking her fourth year of art at Sycamore High School. She has already been accepted to college where she plans to study art. She ultimately wants to be an art teacher, mainly because of her art teacher, Mrs. Stevenson's, influence and guidance.

The art class that she is currently taking is more of a self-directed study. There are a total of five students in the class, and it is obvious to Skylar that they are only in the class because they feel it will be an easy A for them. Mrs. Stevenson allows the students to work at their own pace, but they must compile a portfolio of art as part of their final project and grade.

Two times now, Skylar has come to class only to find that her artwork has been damaged and it is obvious that it was done on purpose. Skylar has an idea of who the culprit is, but has no hard evidence. She mentioned this to Mrs. Stevenson on both occasions, but unfortunately, since Mrs. Stevenson has not witnessed the act, there is not much she can do. A couple of the students were suspiciously quiet when Skylar brought this to Mrs. Stevenson's attention. Skylar is frustrated, very frustrated, because she has had to start over multiple times.

Skylar has worked really hard to get caught up on her work and decides to go back to the art room to get her work and take it home. When Skylar gets to the room, no one is around. She recognizes the artwork of the students whom she suspects have damaged her artwork. The stage is set for payback and revenge.

Discussion Questions:
- There's an old saying, "Revenge is a dish that is best served cold." What do you think this means? Why?

- What if Skylar had proof of who damaged her art projects? Should this make a difference in her decision to damage their art? Why or why not?

- What if Skylar damaged their artwork and then learned that she was wrong about who had damaged her artwork?

- What if the other students report Skylar to Mrs. Stevenson for damaging their artwork? What if Skylar decides to damage their artwork and gets caught?

- What advice would you give to Skylar as to how to handle the situation? What would you do if you were Skylar?

- What, if any, connection do you see between Skylar's story and Joseph's story? What would you have done if you had been in Joseph's position? What advice would you have given Joseph?

Plagues and Passover:
Bugs and Frogs and Blood—Oh My!
by Chris Warren

Scripture: Exodus 7:14–12:30

Theme: The plagues were God's use of power for the benefit of the Israelites.

Resource List

- Paper
- Lemonade made with salt instead of sugar
- Cups
- Pitcher of fresh water
- Writing Utensils
- Newsprint or dry erase board
- Markers or dry erase markers
- Copies of "A Summary of the Ten Plagues" for each student.
- A meeting space that can be made very dark
- Bibles

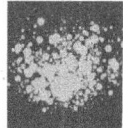

Leader Prep

- Prepare a room where the lights can be turned off. In order to make the room as dark as possible, secure dark posterboard or sheets over any windows or openings that cannot be closed off from light.
- Make copies of "A Summary of the Ten Plagues for each student.
- Prepare the lemonade made with salt instead of sugar.

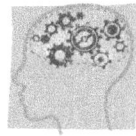

Leader Insight

Connecting to Your Students
Our world is ever shrinking, and people are confronted at almost every turn with people who are very different from them. People sometimes choose to dislike those who are different simply because they are different. But this approach does not affirm that all people are made in God's image, which is a non-negotiable truth that Christians have from scripture.

Teens understand differences all too often when they are faced with those who bully others to get ahead or to boost their own ego or agenda. However, it is difficult for them to reconcile the need to speak up to those who are bullies with the need not to be different for fear of being rejected.

Notes:

Explaining the Bible

From the burning bush, God called Moses to lead the Hebrew people out of slavery in Egypt. (See Exodus 3.) Moses went to the pharaoh and asked for their release. When Pharaoh refused to let the Hebrew people go, God sent ten plagues upon Pharaoh's land. The first six, which included red river water, hordes of frogs, insects and disease, nearly destroyed the land, but still Pharaoh refused to free the Hebrew slaves. The next three plagues brought hail, locusts, and darkness. Then the final, mysterious tenth plague killed all the firstborn humans and animals of Egypt.

The story of the plagues and the first passover of the Israelites contains some very difficult theological questions, many of which do not have easy answers. These passages were written solely from the perspective of the Israelites.

As we approach this topic, there are some difficult issues to address. Why was it okay for the Egyptians to suffer during this time? Why would God harden the heart of Pharaoh if it was going to mean more suffering for the people? Why would it be okay with God for all of the firstborn of the entire nation to die, even if it was for the good of the chosen people?

These are questions that can hardly be answered. Sometimes the best we can do is present the scripture and explain that some of the questions we have are simply mysteries. Yet, the scripture is there to attempt to teach us that God will always take care of the people. Whatever means are necessary, God will save the chosen people.

Authorship of the first five books of the Bible is debatable, but the best scholarship we have now suggests that the stories were finally written down during the Babylonian Exile, around 586-546 B.C.E. If this is true, then the stories would have been especially powerful for the people who were once again being held captive by another nation.

But these accounts don't mean that God is okay with one group using or destroying another group for personal or political benefit. Although the horrors of the plagues that were visited upon the Egyptians were a means to giving the Israelites their freedom, we cannot assume that God intends for us to use similar means to give ourselves authority over other groups or nations. We are a part of the story of God's chosen people, and we do have God's love and support, but there are some extreme differences in culture and context that should give us pause before we interpret this scripture as if we are the Israelites and those who are different from us are the Egyptians.

First, the Israelites were enslaved. At the time the scripture for this lesson begins, the Israelites were being treated terribly and worked harshly. Their destiny to become the people God had called them to be was impeded by their inability to determine their own future.

But even that rationale doesn't answer some of the tough theological questions about suffering and death that the plagues bring up. We will address these questions, but will allow youth to make their own determinations about how to digest the passages.

Whatever your ideas going into this lesson, try to be as open as possible to the youth as they work through the questions. These stories are familiar to many of us, but most of us have seldom dealt with their implications in more than a childlike way. The violence within these stories and the fear and grief that would have been so difficult for the Egyptians are often overlooked when we first hear the stories. And we want to remember what the stories seem to be teaching us, that God is powerful and God will work for justice for those whom God loves.

Theological Underpinnings
In Getting Started, students will be introduced to the plagues through experiential learning, and by quiz, drawing upon what they remember about the ten plagues upon Egypt.

In Listen up, students will explore the plagues, what they were, how they affected the Egyptians, as well as the Israelites, and how God preapred his people to move from the only land they knew to a new land promised to them.

In exploring Pharoah's hardened heart, students will discuss oppression in the time of Moses, as well as today. They will have the option of creating a plan of action to eleviate oppression in their areas and look for ways to share God's love with all people.

Applying the Lesson to Your Own Life
As you meet people, you need to do your best to affirm their humanity and their importance to God. John's Gospel reminds us that God sent the Son so that the entire world—not just certain peoples—might be saved through him.

Notes:

Notes:

Were you ever the one others considered to be different? Did you ever experience ridicule? Or, were you the one who treated others differently? Have you found reconciliation since that time in your life?

What are your own thoughts on suffering and God's will? Does God cause people to suffer in order to accomplish God's will? Think about these questions as you prepare to enter into discussion with your students.

The Lesson

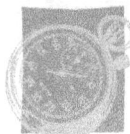

Get Started (25 min.)

Read Exodus Chapter 3, as a group, for background with your students.

Experiential Learning

To help your youth learn a little about the plagues, allow them to experience two of them in a very simple manner. First, make lemonade for the beginning of the lesson, but use salt instead of sugar. Once they have taken a sip, explain that although they have the taste of of nasty lemonade in their mouths, they have sources of water that have not been contaminated. However, the plague of blood that affected the Nile River was not just a bad taste. It made the source of water for the entire country unusable. They had no water for drinking, bathing, irrigating, etc. Egypt is a very hot, arid country; water is essential for people and animals to avoid dehydration. Add to this the death of all the water creatures, and the entire area would have been disgusting, smelly, and completely repulsive.

Turn out all of the lights and block out as much light as possible in your meeting area to begin the next plague experience. This experience may be fun for a couple of minutes, but try giving the youth simple instructions to move around the room or change seats. They will quickly realize that total darkness would stop the functioning of the entire society. There would be little, if anything, they could do. For them, it is clear that the teacher has simply turned out the lights. For the Egyptians, it would have meant the end of the sun, or even the end of the world. The panic would have been widespread, and the fear would have been overwhelming.

How Many Plagues?

Challenge the youth to name the ten plagues as recounted in the Book of Exodus.

Make this a quiz by having each student list the plagues on a sheet of paper or divide into teams. If you have a small group, they may prefer to work together to see how many they can name. For an extra challenge, have the youth list them in the order they occurred.

Once they have completed the challenge, uncover a newsprint or write the following on a dry erase board.

The Ten Plagues of Egypt:
The Plague of Blood (Turning the Nile to Blood): Exodus 7:14-24
The Plague of Frogs: Exodus 7:25-8:15
The Plague of Gnats: Exodus 8:16-8:19
The Plague of Flies: Exodus 8:20-8:32
The Plague on Livestock: Exodus 9:1-9:7
The Plague of Boils: Exodus 9:8-9:12
The Plague of Hail: Exodus 9:13-9:35
The Plague of Locusts: Exodus 10:1-10:20
The Plague of Darkness: Exodus 10:21-29
The Plague of the Firstborn: Exodus 11:1-12:30

Listen Up (20 min.)

The Bible uses several verses to tell about each plague, which means that it would take a long time to read the actual scripture. Therefore, a summary of the plages is available on the handout at the end of this lesson.

Have a volunteer read aloud Exodus 5:1-7 for a brief back

Notes:

Notes:

ground of the story. Then, have someone read aloud Exodus 9:12 in which scripture tells us that God hardened Pharaoh's heart.

Give each student a copy of the handout "A Summary of the Ten Plagues." Invite students to take turns reading aloud one or more of the summaries.

Say: *God had told the people to be ready to move, and they had packed bread and provisions for a journey. Soon after the death of the firstborn, Pharaoh commanded the Israelites to leave Egypt and never come back.*

Now What? (15 min.)

Discussion Questions:
- If you had been one of the Israelite slaves, how do you think you would have felt as these events played out?
- What would you have hoped would be the final outcome?
- How would you have felt if you had been an Egyptian citizen?

Say: *We can imagine that most Egyptians had little or nothing to do with whether or not the Israelites were freed.*

- Is it fair that all of the Egyptians endured such severe punishment? Why or why not?

Say: *Chapter 9, verse 12 states "But the LORD hardened the heart of Pharaoh, and he would not listen to them, just as the LORD had spoken to Moses."*

Over the course of these different plagues, Pharaoh spoke to Moses several times. Moses warned Pharaoh about the consequences each time, but he and his people continued to suffer because Pharaoh hardened his heart and would not let the people go. This time scripture tells us that the LORD hardened Pharaoh's heart so that he would not let the people leave.

Discussion Questions:
- What do you think it means that God hardened

Pharaoh's heart?
- What could be gained by Pharaoh not letting the people go?
- Does it bother you to realize that God hardened Pharaoh's heart, which caused the Egyptian people to endure more plagues? Why or why not?
- What do you think we are supposed to learn from this passage of scripture?

We learn in this story that under extreme circumstances, God is willing to go to great lengths to protect the people God loves. In this case, it was the Israelites. It could be another group of people at another time.

Discussion Question:
- What peoples in our world are being oppressed today?

Say: *Many nations and peoples throughout the world are sometimes oppressed and are sometimes the oppressors. God intends for all people to have an abundant life, and this excludes no one.*

Discussion Questions:
- How can we look for and work against oppression in our world?
- What types of oppression do you see in your lives or in the news?
- What could our youth group do? ("Nothing" is not an acceptable answer.)

Live It (5 min.)

As a closing activity, have your students brainstorm ways they can make a difference locally, in church, in schools, or maybe even on a broader scale. Working to end oppression is never done in vain.

Close the lesson in prayer.

© 2012 Discipleship Ministry Team of the Ministry Council of the Cumberland Presbyterian Church. All Rights Reserved.

JUST IN CASE

Encourage students to spend some time each day reading newspaper headlines, observing the world around them, or in some other way looking for ways that people are oppressed in a local or global setting. It could be as simple as the way products are advertised; it could be as local as the way your town deals with homelessness; or it could be as grand as a totalitarian government in a foreign land. Have them design a plan of action to publicize the need they see or to organize help for that need. Have the students bring these back to the group and work together for a solution. It is amazing what even a small group can do when they work together.

A Summary of the Ten Plagues
PART I

The plague of blood:
When Pharaoh refused to let the Israelites go, God instructed Moses to meet Pharaoh at the river when he went down in the morning to get water. God told Moses to have Aaron, Moses' brother, hold his staff and stretch out his hand over the water. All of the water in the entire nation turned into blood. All the fish died, and there was no water to drink in all of Egypt. After Moses and Aaron had done this, the Egyptian magicians were somehow also able to do it. Pharaoh hardened his heart and would not let the people go.

The plague of frogs:
A week after the plague of blood, Moses went to Pharaoh and told him that if he didn't let the people go, he would bring frogs to cover the entire land. When Pharaoh did not change his mind, Aaron stretched his hand over the waters and frogs came out of them. They came into the homes of the Egyptians and onto their beds. Finally Pharaoh asked Moses to pray to God that the frogs would be taken away. He did, and the frogs went away, but Pharaoh still would not let the people go.

The plague of gnats:
God commanded Moses to have Aaron strike the dust of the ground, and it became gnats flying everywhere in the air and on the people and on their animals. Even the magicians told Pharaoh that this was the finger of God, but Pharaoh's heart was hard and he would not listen.

The plague of flies:
God again commanded Moses to meet Pharaoh on his way down to the river. Moses told Pharaoh that God was going to cover the entire area of Egypt with flies. They would be in every house, in the Pharaoh's palace, and cover the ground. But this time, God made a distinction; the flies did not go to the place where the Israelites lived, the area known as Goshen. (The other plagues had affected the Israelites as well as the Egyptians.) This time Pharaoh told Moses that the people could leave to worship God, but after Moses prayed for the flies to go away (and they did), Pharaoh changed his mind.

The plague of livestock (also called the plague of pestilence):
Moses met with Pharaoh and told him that God commanded him to release the people to worship God. If not, Moses warned that a terrible plague would come upon the livestock of the pharaoh. When Pharaoh did not let the people go, all of the animals belonging to the Egyptians died, but none of the animals belonging to the Israelites died. Pharaoh still would not let the people go.

The plague of boils:
The Lord commanded Moses and Aaron to take some soot from a furnace and throw it into the air in front of Pharaoh. When Moses did this, boils came up on all of the Egyptians and all of their animals. Scholars aren't sure which animals these were; maybe the Egyptians had taken the Israelites' animals or there had been time to buy new animals. This time, scripture tells us that God hardened Pharaoh's heart so that he would not let the people go.

A Summary of the Ten Plagues
PART II

The plague of hail:
God commanded Moses to go to Pharaoh and warn him that although he had not heeded the plagues to that point, he should let the people go immediately or a new and terrible plague would befall the people of Egypt. Moses even told Pharaoh that the plague would be the worst hailstorm Egypt had ever seen. Some of the Egyptians feared what God would do; they placed their animals and slaves under shelter, but others didn't.

The next day hail and thunder struck every part of Egypt except Goshen, where the Israelites lived. It was much worse than any storm Egypt had ever seen. Pharaoh told Moses that Pharaoh and his people had sinned, and that the people could go. Moses agreed to pray for the storm to stop once he had left the city. Moses did as he promised, but once the hail and thunder stopped, Pharaoh hardened his heart again and would not let the people go.

The plague of locusts:
The Lord told Moses at the beginning of this chapter that it was the Lord who had hardened Pharaoh's heart. God explained that this was so that all the people would see the signs and wonders and tell their children and grandchildren for many generations to come how God had dealt with the Egyptians.

Then God threatened to bring locusts on the entire country to devour and destroy everything that the hail had left behind if Pharaoh would not let the Israelites go to worship God. Pharaoh's officials advised Pharaoh simply to let them go, but Pharaoh asked Moses just who would be going. Moses answered that all the old and young, men and women would go. And Pharaoh said no, only the men could go.

The next day, locusts covered the land and devoured every plant in Egypt. Again Pharaoh called Moses and said that he and his people had sinned. He asked Moses to pray for the locusts to leave. Moses did as Pharaoh requested, but again the Lord hardened Pharaoh's heart and Pharaoh did not let the people go.

The plague of darkness:
God then commanded Moses to stretch out his hand and darkness would cover the earth. Moses did as God said, and all Egypt, except the places where the Israelites lived, were totally dark for three days. Pharaoh summoned Moses and again said that he had sinned. He told Moses to take the people, even the women, but to leave their livestock. But Moses refused, telling Pharaoh that they needed the livestock to offer their sacrifices. Again the Lord hardened Pharaoh's heart, and he wouldn't let the people go. Pharaoh threatened Moses and told him never to come to see him again, or Pharaoh would have him killed. Moses agreed and said Pharaoh would never see his face again.

The plague of the firstborn:
God told Moses that there was to be one more plague on the Egyptians. This time, God said, they will not only allow you to leave, they will force you to leave. God told Moses to have the people ask for gold and other precious things from their Egyptian neighbors, who would give it willingly. Then God told Moses what would happen.

That night, the spirit of the Lord would come through the land of Egypt and kill the firstborn of every person, free or slave, and even the firstborn of the livestock. The Israelites were to make a sacrifice to God and place some of the blood on the door frames of their homes. The Spirit of God passed over the homes with the blood on the door frame, but entered the homes and killed the firstborn of every family in Egypt, even the firstborn of the livestock.

The Original Pretty Woman
by Chris Warren

Scripture: Joshua 2 and 4

Theme: God uses strange means to accomplish good. God used Rahab, a prostitute, to protect the Israelite spies and to ultimately defeat Jericho. She is rewarded for faith in the God of Israel.

Resource List

- Items that can be used to create a building and a fence (playing cards, index cards, blocks, etc.)
- Marshmallows
- Plastic Spoons
- Song: "Joshua Fit The Battle of Jericho"
- Music player (laptop, iPod, MP3 player, CD player, speakers, etc.)
- Bibles
- Copies of the handout for each student

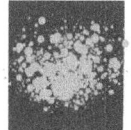

Leader Prep

- Song: "Joshua Fit The Battle of Jericho." It is available on YouTube at http://www.youtube.com/watch?v=Ks7fLAwzVxY. There are many other great recordings of this piece. If you prefer to use a different version, do a YouTube or Google search.
- An alternative to using "Joshua Fit the Battle of Jericho" is Veggie Tales' "Keep Walking, but You Won't Knock Down Our Wall."

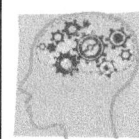

Leader Insight

Connecting to Your Students
There are two main themes in this lesson. First is the way that God used a prostitute named Rahab as a major player in the success of the Israelite people's campaign against Jericho. Second, is the way that the people of Israel defeated Jericho. Both of these themes are part of an overarching story that has been playing out through the exodus and now continues into the military campaign to take over the promised land: God is working on behalf of the Israelites, and even if odds are against them, if they act in faith, they will succeed. This means they must do what God says even when it seems to make no sense.

Notes:

Your students more than likely have a poor view of those who work as prostitutes. This lesson is not intended to glorify the profession of prostitution, but it does show us that God can (and does) use people from all backgrounds in executing God's plan. Sometimes young people have a hard time understanding that God has a plan for them, or that they could be used in any way to further God's plan and kingdom. Each and every one of us, regardless of our past, can be an instrument of God.

Explaining the Bible

Prostitution has never been an honorable profession, but in the ancient near east it was significantly different than how we view it today. There were no laws against prostitution. Prostitutes always lived in the less-than-desirable parts of a city, such as within the wall itself. Such women were not the type of peope with whom society's upper crust would deal in the daytime. In many ways prostitutes, then as now, were treated very badly. But in some ways the role of prostitute actually gave a woman more autonomy in the society. For example, most women in this time period were the "property" of the men in their lives. They couldn't even sign a contract on their own behalf. A legal document had to have the signature of a husband, father, or adult male child. Exceptions included prostitutes and widows with no other relations.

The prostitute was also considered a necessary function in the society in which the ancients lived. Men took ownership of all things, including women, and looking at Jewish law of the time, we know that to "know" another man's wife (or daughter, while she was still his "property") was punishable in severe ways, depending upon the circumstances. But the sexuality of the prostitute, unlike other women, belonged to herself. This was considered a necessary way for men to be "satisfied" if they were unmarried, or even if they were married.

In the film *Pretty Woman*, Julia Roberts' character is found to be the one in a million "harlot with a heart of gold." We can see from the Book of Joshua that this story is not peculiar to late the 20th century American film industry, but has been around for a long time. Perhaps the prostitute's heroism is enhanced because people expect prostitutes to look out only for themselves. Or, perhaps, the cleverness of Rahab, being able to recognize that the Israelites would win the day, is the highlight of the story. Her participation in the story shows us that she alone, a prostitute, was wise beyond the kings of the area who refused to believe that this band of Israelites repre sented a threat.

This story is the first in a number of stories that demonstrate how the Israelites began to assume their promised land. It may sound good for the Israelites, but it is not a pretty picture of a loving society. In fact, the discerning reader will notice that God commands the Israelites not only to take over the places that they fight, but to kill everything within the cities, including all of the people: men, women, and even babies. They are to kill all of the livestock as well. All of it is to be unusable for the Israelites. The gold, silver, and other treasures become property of the priests for use in the future temple of the Israelites.

This reality is difficult for us to imagine. It is one thing to take over a place and have it as your own, but it is another to destroy every living thing within that place in order to purify it for the use of your own people. Sometimes we think of this as racially motivated, but not in this case. It was motivated by a desire for religious purity. No one was allowed to survive and become a part of the people of God for fear that there might be some adoption of their beliefs into the religious beliefs of Israel. Therefore, in order to keep their religion pure, everything must die. It is a horrifying chapter in the history of the people of Israel.

The Israelites march around the city several times blowing trumpets and finally shouting. The walls collapse, except for the part in which Rahab and her family have gathered, allowing the Israelites to enter the city and win the battle.

Theological Underpinnings
In the gathering activity, students will explore how ancient cities used a wall surrounding the city as a method of defense; however, it could also be used as a method of offense.

In "LIsten Up," students will explore the scripture, discussing who Rehab was and how and why God used her.

This lesson will conclude with a discussion of the walls in our lives. We often put up walls between ourselves and others. We will explore how can God help us to tear down the walls that prevent us from living to our full potential in Christ.

Applying the Lesson to Your Own Life
If a prostitute were to enter your church, how would you treat her?

Notes:

Notes:

Have you ever wondered why God called some people to specific ministry? Did you ever think that maybe God chose the wrong person for the job?

Romans 3 states that we all fall short of the glory of God. We are all sinners, but we often consider some sins to be worse than others. In God's eyes, each sin is equal. How can we turn a blind eye to the sin in one another and accept people as children of God whom God has called for a specific purpose?

What walls are interfering with your life? How can God assist in tearing down any kind of "wall" that keeps you from living your life as Christ would want you to live it?

What are your own thoughts on suffering and God's will? Does God cause people to suffer in order to accomplish God's will? Think about these questions as you prepare to enter into discussion with your students.

The Lesson

Get Started (20 min.)

Separate students into teams of three or four with the instructions that they are to build structures around the room to replicate a city with a wall around it. Some building materials are suggested, but whatever you can come up with that is fair to all the youth is perfectly fine. As they are building their "cities," remind them that the city wall was supposed to keep out invaders.

Say: *The city walls were the best protection cities had from aggressive armies. But they also allowed those other armies to lay siege to the cities. In other words, an attacking army outside the walls of the city could keep supplies such as food and water from entering, or keep people or other things like waste materials from leaving the city. Many wars were won with the siege strategy.*

Give a limited amount of time to build the "cities" and their walls.

Explain: *You will now see what it was like to try to breach the walls of a city, except the methods you will use are quite different from the ones used by the Israelites.*

Using the marshmallows as projectiles and the plastic spoons as catapults, let each group, from a specified distance, start launching at the other group's city. Limit the number of projectiles, or continue until one city is only rubble. Just have a good time seeing which city lasts longer.

Celebrate the person/group that knocks down the other's "city wall."

Listen Up (20 min.)

Have students take turns reading aloud Joshua chapter 2.

This chapter contains the story of Rahab. For some reason she was not only willing to allow the men to stay at her home, something that was probably not uncommon given her profession, but somehow she determined that their side was going to win the battle. She was moved to faith in the God of the Israelites, and she was willing to help the Israelite spies, at great risk to herself, against her own people.

Discussion Question:
- What do you think the Israelite spies were doing at Rahab's home?

Say: (See leader tip) *It could be that they were visiting a prostitute for the reason that most men of that time would have visited a prostitute. It is also true that no woman other than a prostitute would have willingly been alone in the same room with them. Her proximity to the gates of the city made her home ideal. It could be that they simply ran into her first.*

Discussion Question:
- Why do you think Rahab decided to help the Israelite spies?

Notes:

Leader Tip:
Proceed with this statement cautiously. Be prepared to bring the group back on track as this could lead to many sidebar conversations.

Notes:

Leader Tip:
More to the Story

Flip to the first chapter of the Gospel of Matthew where you will find the genealogy of Jesus Christ. There are only a few women mentioned in this genealogy, but if you read it closely, you will find Rahab listed in the fifth verse! Not only did God provide for the Israelite spies through this outcast of society, but the very savior of the world is one of her direct descendents. If that doesn't show us how God can work in ways that we might not expect, what does?

Say: *Somehow she recognized that the God they were serving was the real God. She also recognized that somehow they were going to win the battle and destroy Jericho. She very likely simply chose to support them so that when or if they did conquer the city, she and her family would be saved. If everyone in the city was to be slaughtered, it didn't hurt for her to have allegiances on both sides. At any rate, she came to faith in the God of Israel and was rewarded not only with her life, but she and her family become a part of the chosen people because of her faith.*

Salvation for the Israelite spies came through an unlikely source—the prostitute Rahab. God truly does do things in unexpected ways.

Discussion Question:
- What might we learn from the way God chose to rescue the spies?

Say: *God can offer redemption in many, many ways. We might not even recognize it or choose to look in the direction God offers our redemption if we were not in serious trouble like the Israelite spies.*

The Battle

Play the recording of "Joshua Fit the Battle of Jericho."

The following commentary is about the composition of the piece, written by the arranger, Moses Hogan.

"Joshua Fit the Battle of Jericho" is an African-American Spiritual. It is thought to have been composed by slaves in the American South who were taught Christianity in the generations after their capture and sale into the slave trade in the Americas. Like many of the African-American Spirituals, the emphasis is on the rescue given by God in a miraculous way and against the odds as they would have been understood. Who expects that the walls will fall down because people march around and blow trumpets and shout? But the walls did come down, and for the slaves who sang this song to one another, whether they were working in the fields or were in their lodgings, it gave them hope that the walls of the institution that kept them in bondage would one day be thrown down as completely and miraculously as the walls of the city that the Israelites destroyed in the Book of Joshua.

Unbelievable Means

Read Joshua chapter 6.

The group of Israelites had more or less been a band of wandering foragers rather than a military force. But they had obviously been making plans to take over the land that God had promised to their ancestor Abraham many generations earlier. Their first military campaign was against what appeared to be a well-fortified city. Joshua sent spies to see how difficult it would be to overrun the city, at which point then encountered Rahab. God told Joshua how to proceed. When the time came, the great strategy was to march around the city six times, once each day for six days, playing trumpets. On the seventh day they were to march around the city seven times, playing trumpets. At this time the people were to shout and the walls were to come down.

According to Joshua chapter 6, the people did all of this (so much for resting on the seventh day...) and the walls fell down in front of them. They rushed in and destroyed the entire city, leaving nothing behind. They took with them Rahab and her family and the treasures of the city, burning the rest of the city.

God commanded the people to do something that mades no sense—march around and play loud noises and finally shout for the walls to come down. With their history of disobeying God, it is almost a surprise to see that they did exactly what God commanded.

Discussion Questions:
- Why do you think the people, who had been complaining against God and Moses during the Exodus, and who were required to wander for forty years because of their unbelief, were willing to do what God asked of them in this circumstance?
- Have you ever thought or felt that you were being called by God to do something unusual, something that might not make sense? How did you respond?
- How could we use the example of the walls of Jericho to help us to have faith to confront the walls that keep us from what God wants in our lives?

Leader Tip:
God's calling is somehow always going to confirm God's love for us and for all God's people. This confirmation of love doesn't seem to happen at Jericho, but it is a good idea to keep the overall love of God in mind when trying to discern what God is asking of us and to what our humanity may be pulling us.

Jericho: History or Myth?
Archaeological evidence has not only been scarce in confirming the biblical account of the destruction of Jericho, it has shown that there was no city in the ancient location of Jericho at the time of the Israelites' crossing of the Jordan. It is possible that the city was in another location. It is possible that other evidence may come to light that will refute the current knowledge. The location shows that the wall around the city has collapsed multiple times; the most recent collapse seems to have been about nine hundred years before the Israelites would have been there.

JUST IN CASE
History or Myth?

The location of the ancient city of Jericho, however, is a place that is prone to seismic activity like earthquakes. Modern acoustics could account for some type of collapse under the right conditions, especially if the foundation of the wall had been undermined by seismic activity.

How does this information affect you and your students?

If the battle did not happen exactly the way it is described in the Book of Joshua, how does that affect your faith?

What about the possibility of acoustic methods destroying the walls of a city?

Possible Answer:
As with much of scripture, the important thing for us to remember is that it isn't intended to be an impartial history book. It tells a story, and the important thing to remember about this story is that God is on the side of the people. Whether or not the city of Jericho existed in the way it is described in the Book of Joshua, the story teaches that we must have faith in God for our salvation. The New Testament reaffirms this truth as well.

Now What? (15 min.)

The Walls Come Tumblin' Down

This week, take time each night to reflect on the walls in your life. What barriers are keeping you from being who God wants you to be?

Are they walls between you and other people? walls between you and an ability to have faith in God in the way you would like? walls between you and your parents? walls between you and schoolwork?

Take time to write these walls down.

Live It (5 min.)

Pray over these things and remember that if God can destroy the actual walls of a city, God can work through and within you to destroy anything that is keeping you from being the faithful follower of God you want and God wants you to be.

Resources used in this lesson:
Bird, Phyllis, "The Harlot as Heroine" Women in the Hebrew Bible, Alice Bach, ed. (New York, Routledge publishing, 1999), pp 105-109.

Frick, Frank S. A Journey Through The Hebrew Scriptures, 2nd Edition (Wadsworth/Thompson Learning, Belmont, CA, 2003) pp 250-251.

© 2012 Discipleship Ministry Team of the Ministry Council of the Cumberland Presbyterian Church. All Rights Reserved.

My God Rules, your god Drools...
by Chris Warren

Scripture: 1 Kings 18:20-46

Theme: Faithfulness to God is not an option but a requirement for the Israelites. There is only one God, and they should not allow different cultures to influence them otherwise.

Resource List

- Matches or lighter
- Newspaper
- 3 buckets of water
- Pile of sticks
- Optional: Mendelssohn's Oratorio, "Elijah"
- Internet and video capability
- Bibles

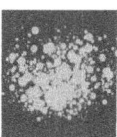

Leader Prep

- If you can, secure a place to try to burn something. See instructions in "Get Started."
- Optional: Mendelssohn's Oratorio, "Elijah" - An extended version can be found at: http://www.youtube.com/watch?v=m6T63kJ9cdY&feature=related.

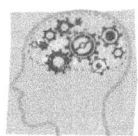

Leader Insight

Connecting to Your Students
Teens are bombarded by dreams of wealth, celebrity, power, or many other things that humans treat as gods. At a very early age young people are given the message that the more you have, the more you have and you will be happy. Some youth think that having more of these "gods" will bring them happiness.

In the case of the worshippers of Ba'al found in 1 Kings 18, the people were not look for their gods to bring them happiness, but save them.

Explaining the Bible
In the Book of Joshua, God commanded the people to eliminate all remnants of other religions in the Promised Land.

Notes:

They were even commanded to kill everyone in the land as conquered the peoples who lived there so that they would not be influenced by other religious groups. The Book of Judges tells us that the people were faithful to God but then fell away. Each time they fell away, God called forth a judge to show them the path back to faithfulness. By the time the first king, Saul, came along, the people had proved themselves pretty fickle in their worship of God. Then David became king, and he was "a man after God's own heart." He was not perfect, but he was steadfast in his worship of the one true God. His successor, Solomon, started out good, but his many, many wives influenced him, and by the time he died there were religious temples and shrines to many different gods in the land of Israel.

After Solomon, there was a struggle for the throne that eventually caused the creation of two different kingdoms—Israel in the north and Judah in the south. Ahab ruled the northern kingdom of Israel from 869-850 B.C.E. Ahab allowed his foreign-born wife, Jezebel, to promote the worship of Baal over the worship of God. Soon Ahab was worshiping Baal, and the people followed his example.

The Book of First Kings introduces the character of Elijah, one of the most important figures in the Old Testament. Many of the miracles Elijah performed are similar to the ones Jesus performed in his ministry. Chapter 17 tells of Elijah miraculously feeding a widow and her son for many days after her food (in this case just oil and flour) should have run out. Compare this to the Gospel stories of Jesus feeding thousands of people from a meager amount of food. Later in the same chapter, Elijah used the power of the Lord to revive the widow's dead son. Again, we can compare this to Jesus raising the daughter of the Temple official Jairus and raising his friend Lazarus, both of whom had died.

The story of the Transfiguration (Luke 9:28-36) helps us to understand just how highly the Jewish people revered Elijah. Jesus took Peter, James, and John with him when he went up on the mountain to pray. While he was praying, the appearance of his face changed and his clothes became dazzling white. The disciples saw Jesus talking to two other men whom they recognized as Moses and Elijah. Out of all the great founders of the faith, the two people Jesus was seen talking with at his transfiguration were Moses and Elijah! This tells us just how important Elijah and his story were to the Jews of Jesus' time.

Because Ahab and Jezebel were worshiping idols, especially the god Baal, the prophets of the Lord were persecuted and in great danger. Elijah was a great prophet of the Lord, but much of the time he lived in hiding because of the threat from Ahab and Jezebel. First Kings 18 tells of the need to hide many of the prophets of God. The prophets of Baal were safe and sound, and apparently healthy in number.

Chapter 18 of First Kings brings to an end the battle between God and Baal over rain. In 17:1 Elijah announced that there would be no rain except by God's word. Baal, the god of the storms, would be powerless by the word from God. The story in 1 Kings 18:20-46 took place during a period of great drought in the land. If ever it was a good time to try to burn anything, this was it. After blocking the rain clouds for three years, God sent Elijah to Ahab with the word that God would send rain to the land again. A showdown was about to take place on Mt. Carmel.

There were apparently about four hundred and fifty priests of Baal, all crying out to him and asking him to burn the offering they had left. They even resorted to screaming and cutting themselves to try to get the attention of the god in which they believed.

Elijah wasn't very nice about their failure. He let this go on for hours and hours while the priests of Baal became more and more frenzied. He even said their god must be sleeping, and when he mentioned that the god might have "wandered away," (vs. 27) he was referring to a Hebrew saying that meant he went to relieve himself.

Theological Underpinnings

The opening activity "Making A Fire" will connect your student to what Elijah was trying to accomplish, first hand. Building a fire over soaked timber or kindling is impossible. It will solidify the point that nothing is impossible with God.

In "Listen Up," students will delve into the scripture lesson, exploring how Elijah might have felt and thought as he watched the worshippers of Baal fail in their attempt to one-up God.

The session will conclude with a prayer of Elijah, remembering not to be like the Israelites of so many years and forget God or to try and worship other things in our lives. We are God's and God is the recipient of our worship.

Notes:

Applying the Lesson to Your Own Life

What kind of fake gods do people serve in this day and age? What do we seek from those "gods"? How do we cry out for help or attention from those "gods"?

Have you ever caught yourself going after a fake god that you thought would bring you happiness? How did you handle it? Were you able to turn from it on your own? with help?

What do you think of Elijah's way of dealing with the priests of Baal?

Have you ever been the Elijah in the story, urging friends or family to turn from their fake gods? How did you approach that situation? What things would you do differently?

The Lesson

Get Started (10 min.)

Making a Fire

If you can, secure a place to burn something. Gather matches or a lighter, newspaper, and three buckets of water.

Make a pile of sticks with newspaper at the bottom and then tell the kids that you are going to light a fire for the lesson. Pour the three buckets of water over the pile of sticks. This experience will be even more effective if the "pit" actually contains standing water.

Then try to light the paper. Be careful with this activity!

Obviously, the wet paper and sticks won't light. Muse aloud to yourself about how surprised you are that the fire material won't burn. Finally give up, frustrated, and move to the scripture lesson.

Listen Up (20 min.)

Read 1 Kings 18:20-29.

Discussion Question:
- What's going on here?

Ask the students to put the scripture into their own words.

- When Elijah says that the people are "limping with two different opinions" (vs. 21) what does he mean?

Say: *The people have been moving back and forth between worshiping the LORD and worshiping Baal. They have been swayed by the new group of priests and by their king, which is not surprising. People usually listen to and follow those who are in authority. The people were admonished but not judged in the same way that the prophets of Baal were.*

Discussion Questions:
- What kind of fake gods do people serve today?
- What are people seeking from those "gods"?
- How do we cry out for help or attention from those "gods"?

In the case of those who believed in Baal, they thought the idol was an actual deity who would save them. Most of us think that something else all together will save us.

Say: *Elijah wasn't very nice about the priest's failure to get Baal to send down fire on their sacrifice. Elijah let their frenzied activity continue for hours and hours. He even said that their god must be sleeping, and when he mentioned that the god might have "wandered away," (vs. 27) he was using a Hebrew saying that means he went to relieve himself.*

Read 1 Kings 18:30-40.

Say: *Elijah waited for hours before responding. Then, he made it seem that God could not possibly prevail. The wood for the sacrifice was soaked with buckets of water—during a time of great drought and need for water! The ground was not only soaked, there was standing water at the bottom of the altar on which the sacrifice had been placed.*

But Elijah didn't dance around the place, he didn't scream, he

Leader Tip:

The scripture in this lesson speaks of the priest's of Baal cutting themselves. Cutting is a serious issue among young people. Here is some information for you regarding cutting, if questions were to arise.

Injuring yourself on purpose by making scratches or cuts on your body with a sharp object — enough to break the skin and make it bleed — is called cutting. Cutting is a type of self-injury, or SI. Most people who cut are girls, but guys self-injure, too. People who cut usually start cutting in their young teens. Some continue to cut into adulthood.

People may cut themselves on their wrists, arms, legs, or bellies. Some people self-injure by burning their skin with the end of a cigarette or lighted match.

When cuts or burns heal, they often leave scars or marks. People who injure themselves usually hide the cuts and marks and sometimes no one else knows.

Cutting is a way some people try to cope with the pain of strong emotions, intense pressure, or upsetting relationship problems. They may be dealing with feelings that seem too difficult to bear or bad situations they think can't change.

Some people cut because they feel desperate for relief from bad feelings. People who cut may not know better ways to get relief from emotional pain or pressure. Some people cut to express strong feelings of rage, sorrow, rejection, desperation, longing, or emptiness.

If your young people or know someone they know is using cutting as a way to cope help them to get the help they need to deal with issues in a healthy manner.

JUST IN CASE
Re-read 1 Kings 18:46

This type of thing happens to Elijah a lot in the story. In verses 7-16, Elijah is said to have appeared and disappeared several times in many different places. These appearances are attributed to the Spirit of the Lord. At the end of the book, Elijah runs back to the entrance of Jezreel, arriving before Ahab who is riding in a chariot. Strange, huh? What point is the writer trying to make?

Possible Answer: Elijah has special powers because of his special relationship with and faithfulness to God. The mention of these incidents is intended to set him apart as special even among those who serve God.

The Gospels also tell of Jesus doing some of the special things first recorded about Elijah. Sometimes Jesus appeared in special, incredible circumstances such as when he walked on water in Matthew 6:45-52. Another time he slipped through an entire crowd when many of those in the crowd were looking for him to grab him (Luke 4:28-30).

---

certainly didn't cut himself. He simply prayed that God would show that God was real. The one true God, the God of Israel responded immediately. The sacrifice, the wood, the water—even the rocks—were consumed by a fire that scripture tells us fell from heaven.

Ask students to spend some time imagining.
- Imagine being in that place at that time. What do you see, smell, feel, hear?
- Imagine yourself as one of the people who had been swayed by the priests of Baal. What is going through your mind?
- Now imagine that you are one of the priests of Baal. What are you thinking?

Say: *If you were one of the priests of Baal, you didn't have much time to think. Elijah told the people to seize the prophets of Baal and then killed them almost immediately. How do you feel about this type of ending to the prophets of Baal?*

- What bothers you most about this story?

Read 1 Kings 18:41-46.

Say: *Because the people turned back to faith in the one true God, salvation came to them. In this case, salvation came in the form of rain that fell to the earth. Droughts are always serious, but just imagine how much more serious they would have been in the ancient world. The weather patterns wwere often interpreted as God's faithfulness or lack of faithfulness to the people.*

Discussion Questions:
- What do you expect will happen in the following chapters? How will it affect Ahab? Elijah?

Now What? (15 min.)

The story isn't over for Elijah, but he is in a much better place than he was at the beginning of this chapter. Ahab, on the other hand, is much worse off, even with the falling of the rain. Jezebel decided to try to have Elijah killed, but eventually things worked out well for Elijah. Jezebel died horribly, and God whisked Elijah off to heaven as one of only two people who never died.

Discussion Questions:
- What do you like about this story? What bugs you? With what do you struggle?
- What about the expectation for a grand sign from heaven? We often do not receive these kinds of signs that God is present, but our faith is supposed to be as strong as Elijah's.
- How do we continue to keep our faith strong when we read about miraculous occurrences such as these and many of us never witness one?

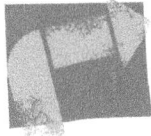

Live It (5 min.)

Ask students to join you in the following *"Prayer in the Spirit and Power of Elijah."*

> O LORD, the God of Abraham, Isaac and Israel,
> You alone are God.
> Your servant Elijah lived in your presence,
> and acted on your Word.
> Help us to drink from the well of his wisdom.
> Shelter us in Cherith, and lead us to Carmel,
> luring our hearts away from all false gods.
> Open our eyes to the needs of those who are suffering.
> Open our mouths to speak comfort and justice.
> Open our hearts to your voice in the silence.
> Send angels to strengthen us.
> Send the rain of your grace to quench our thirst.
> Let us break bread with the starving
> and bring life to places of death and despair.
> Send us as prophets to herald your gospel.
> Allow us to rise to you in paradise.
> Those who met your son Jesus saw in him
> the spirit of Elijah.
> May Elijah lead us to your son.
> We ask this in Jesus' name. Amen.

Resources used: www.carmelite.org. (The prayer is inspired by the Elijah narratives in the Book of 1 Kings.)

© 2012 Discipleship Ministry Team of the Ministry Council of the Cumberland Presbyterian Church. All Rights Reserved.

JUST IN CASE

Listen to a recording of part of Mendelssohn's Oratorio, "Elijah." An oratorio is a piece of music written for a solo voice and choir with orchestra. Mendelssohn wrote "Elijah" in 1846. Of special interest in the oratorio is a chorus entitled "Baal, We Cry to Thee." It is a depiction of the prophets of Baal crying out to their "god" for help and for a sign of his existence. It is about three minutes long, and is available on youtube. An extended version can be found at: http://www.youtube.com/watch?v=m6T63kJ9cdY&feature=related.

It's About Love, Not a Big Fish
by Samantha Hassell

Scripture: Jonah 1–4

Theme: The message of God's love and goodness is meant for all people. It is not up to us as God's followers to decide who is worthy of God's love. We are to be obedient to God's call, have compassion for all people, and share God's love with everyone we encounter.

Resource List

- Newsprint or erasable board
- Four puzzle pieces as described in "Leader Prep"
- Poster board
- Markers
- A copy of the "Agape" handout for each student
- Laptop
- Video capabilities
- Dr. Martin Luther King, Jr., video

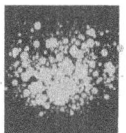

Leader Prep

- During "Listen Up" students will receive a puzzle piece. Create these puzzle pieces out of poster board. Take two sheets of poster board and cut two "puzzle shapes" out of each of them so that you have a total of four pieces. The individual pieces will need to fit together like a puzzle. Write one of the following on each piece: "Chapter 1," "Chapter 2," "Chapter 3," and "Chapter 4."
- During "Live It" students will view a speech made by Dr. Martin Luther King, Jr. Sccess this speech by going to www.wingclips.com and then typing "not like...love" in the search box. This video is 1:20 minutes. You may wish to have students view the clip or just listen to the speech. View it ahead of time to have it cued and ready.

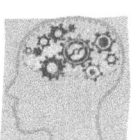

Leader Insight

Connecting to Your Students
Young people crave independence. And rightly so. As the adults who love them, we encourage, offer, and look for ways to let them exercise independence. And while teenagers yearn for independence, they also must follow directions. Coaches, teachers, parents, etc. are all telling them what to do, when

Notes:

to do it, and how long they can do it. When put this way, you can understand why young people can be frustrated! Ultimately, they don't want to follow anyone's directions but their own. We want to help them understand that exerting their independence and following God's call are not separate, that our desire as disciples is not to go our own way, but to follow God's way. Even when God's way leads us to encounter situations or people that we wish to avoid.

Explaining the Bible

The story of Jonah and the big fish is one of the most well-known Old Testament stories. But we do Jonah and his story an injustice when we only know him as the guy in the fish's belly. Jonah's story is one of obedience; of God's love for God's people no matter who they are or what they've done; and of God's compassion and grace. Throw in a vacation stay in the belly of a great fish and a vine eating worm and it's also a cool story!

Jonah's story begins approximately fifty years or so after Elisha's ministry. (To read more regarding the prophet Elisha, read 1Kings 19:19-21.) Israel was being threatened by the Assyrians, whose capital was Nineveh. The Assyrians were known for their power and cruelty, which is why God sent Jonah to tell the people of Nineveh and Assyria that they needed to repent. Jonah, as you may know, said, "No." Jonah didn't resist because he feared for his life or because the trip would be too much. Jonah resisted because he knew of the nature of God. Jonah feared that the people of Nineveh would indeed repent and turn from their evil ways and when they did he trusted that God would forgive and bless them. Jonah hated the Assyrians. He sought vengeance, not mercy.

Jonah wasn't interested in spreading God's love to this nation of people. So Jonah ran and, in his running, ended up in the belly of a great fish which was sent not to end Jonah's life but to spare it. While in the belly of the fish, Jonah came to his senses, found himself back on dry land, and went immediately to preach to the people of Nineveh. The Ninevites did indeed repent and, just as Jonah had expected, received God's compassion. You'd think Jonah would've learned, but even still he grew angry over the Lord's compassion. The Book of Jonah is full of God's love and provision. God spared the sailors. God spared Jonah. God spared the 120,000 plus people who lived in Nineveh. God provided a fish, some shade, and a worm all to help Jonah, God's prophet, understand first hand that God loves and cares for all of us whether we are a nation of evil-doers or a disobedient prophet.

After the repentance of the Ninevites, Jonah complained to God, was rebuked by God, and went out of the city to watch, wait, and see what would happen. As Jonah sat, God provided a fast growing vine to shade and cool Jonah. And the very next morning, God provided a worm to eat the vine, leaving Jonah exposed to the elements.

God's response to Jonah's anger is the point to the story. God had spared Jonah's life when he was disobedient and God continued to provide for him even after he had voiced his resentment toward God. God had saved the people of Nineveh through Jonah's preaching. Jonah was selfishly concerned about the vine because it shaded him, but he had no compassion for the thousands of folks in Nineveh who needed to know God. When Jonah whined about the loss of the vine, which God had provided, God had had enough! "But the LORD said, 'You have been concerned about this vine, though you did not tend it or make it grow. It sprang up overnight. But Nineveh has more than 120,000 people who cannot tell their right hand from their left, and many cattle as well. Should I not be concerned with that great city?'" God loves all God's people, even the ones who are not like us; God calls us to show compassion in the same way that God does.

Theological Underpinnings

Students will open the session by considering some of the sin and evil in the world, zeroing in on groups guilty of said evils and their feelings about those types of people. The goal is to help young people understand why Jonah refused to go to Nineveh.

Students will then work as a team to put together the story of Jonah for one another. They will learn about agape love and God's call for us to express such love to those around us regardless of whether or not we think they deserve it. Students will end with a prayer asking God to help them be willing to share agape love.

Applying the Lesson to Your Own Life

As you prepare to lead this study, re-read the Book of Jonah in its entirety with fresh eyes. Reading a translation other than the one with which you are most familiar can provide new insights into scripture. Make note of the things you learn. Maybe you learned this story as a child but have skimmed over it as an adult, thinking you knew it fully. What jumps out to you as you read it with a new vision? What new learning's do you wish to pass on to your young people?

Notes:

Notes:

What does compassion look like to you? Could it mean forgiving an enemy or giving to those in need? Compassion takes many faces. How can you be the face of compassion to the people with whom you live in community? Ask God to show you how you can be more compassionate and how to lead your young people to be more compassionate as well.

The Lesson

Get Started (12 min.)

Whom Do Ya Love?

Begin by asking students to create a list of evil, sinful, or wrong things that people do. Record their answers on a sheet of newsprint. After several minutes of brainstorming, or when their responses begin to wane, ask:
- As we created our list, what feelings manifested themselves about the wrongs that have been mentioned?

Next, encourage young people to examine the list, considering the people who commit these wrongs.

Discussion Questions:
- To which of these people would you have the hardest time showing love or kindness? Why?
- Are there wrongs on the list with which you can live? Are there wrongs on the list that completely disgust you?
- Do you think you could have compassion for persons who have committed the wrongs we've listed? Do they deserve compassion? Why or why not?

Explain to your students that some things are recognized across the board as being evil; no one would question it as evil. There are other things that may seem very wrong to some people and not-that-big-of-a-deal to others. Today's scripture shows us a nation of people who had become evil and one of God's prophets who refused to relate to them.

Invite students to tell you everything they can remember about Jonah. After they have brainstormed all that they know, affirm their knowledge and invite them to take a look at the Book of Jonah with you.

Listen Up (20 min.)

The Scripture

Say: *Jonah was one of God's prophets and his story is recorded in the Book of Jonah. However, there's one thing that makes his story different from that of other prophets. When the stories of other prophets are told, the telling focuses greatly on the prophesies—God's message or what God had to say through those prophets. But Jonah's story focuses more on the story of Jonah himself. The Book of Jonah is only four chapters long, so we're going to look at the entire book.*

Divide students to create four groups.

Assign each group one of the four chapters and give the groups the appropriate puzzle piece and some markers.

Have students read the assigned chapter and then highlight the events of that chapter on the puzzle piece. They may draw pictures, write words or phrases, create a brief summary, or a mixture of these options. Invite students to remember key points in their chapter as it will be up to them to fill in that piece of the story for the rest of the group. Give students about 10 minutes to read their passage and create their puzzle piece.

After the allotted time, ask the Chapter 1 group to share what they read and to lay their puzzle piece in the center of the floor. Then invite the Chapter 2 group to share what they read and fit their puzzle piece with Chapter 1's. Do the same with Chapters 3 & 4.

Praise your young people for piecing together Jonah's puzzle.

Leader Tip:
If your group is small, it may mean individuals or pairs reading a chapter; if your group is larger, have groups of 4 or 5.

Leader Tip:
Have each of four groups read one chapter and then put the story together for the total group like a puzzle. If you have fewer than four youth in your total group, assign an additional chapter to one or two students.

Leader Tip:
Offer time reminders throughout the ten minutes.

Leader Tip:
Be very familiar with the story so that you can fill in any spaces that your students overlook.

Notes:

Discussion Questions:
- When Jonah refused to go to Nineveh, who did his disobedience affect?
- Why did Jonah initially refused to visit Nineveh?
- What does Jonah's story teach us about what it means to have compassion on God's people?
- Does Jonah's story change the way you look at the list we made earlier? Why or why not? How do you feel knowing that God calls you to have compassion on all people—even when doing so is difficult for you?

Now What? (15 min.)

Pass out the "Agape" handout.

Invite participants to read the definition of the word *agape* and complete the handout. You may want to work on this handout as a total group.

Say: Agape, *as you see, means unconditional love. It is the type of love that God has for us—it's the type of love Jesus demonstrated, and it's the type of love God asks us to have for others.*

Invite students to think of people throughout history as well as people people they know personally who have demonstrated agape love and list them on their worksheet.

Watch the video clip of Dr. Martin Luther King, Jr.

Discussion Questions:
- How did God invite Jonah to show agape?
- How did Martin Luther King, Jr., promote agape?
- Is loving our enemies the same as showing God's compassion? Why or why not?
- In what ways can you practice agape love?

Live It (5 min.)

Invite students to stand in a circle and close with prayer.

Explain to the students that you will open and close the prayer and they are invited to go around the circle giving each individual the chance to offer a prayer by finishing this sentence: *"Thank you, compassionate God for your love. Help me to show agape by…"*

Resources used: www.dictionary.com; www.wingclips.com; *Westminster Dictionary of Theological Terms*.

© 2012 Discipleship Ministry Team of the Ministry Council of the Cumberland Presbyterian Church. All Rights Reserved.

Notes:

Agape

a•ga•pe [ah-gah-pey] noun

1. the love God or Christ has for humankind.
2. the love of Christians for other persons, corresponding to the love of God for humankind.
3. the unselfish love of one person for another without sexual implications;
4. Love feast
from www.dictionary.com

agape ("love")
The self-giving love seen supremely in God's love for the world (John 3:16) and as a mark of the Christian life (1 Corinthians 13). Also a fellowship meal (love feast) in the early church held in conjunction with or separate from the Lord's Supper.

Those Who Show Agape

_____   _____

_____

_____   _____

_____

Is 2012 the End?
by Andy McClung

Scripture: Matthew 24:36

Theme: People are saying the world will end on December 21, 2012. Where does this idea come from, and what is a Christian to think about it?

Resource List

- Computer or DVD player
- Projector
- Internet and video capability
- Speakers
- Clip from the movie *Big Fish*
- Clip from the movie *2012*

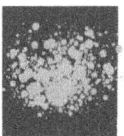

Leader Prep

- Prepare for viewing the scene from the movie *Big Fish* in Chapter 2 of the DVD, 10:08 to 13:26. You can also find it at http://www.youtube.com/watch?v=41J45SvosV0&feature=related. Please cue this clip to 00:30 to avoid any curse words. End the clip at 7:23. Preview the clip before showing to your class.
- Prepare the YouTube video clip "Watch a 5 Minute clip from 2012 - on Blu-ray & DVD." It can be found at http://www.youtube.com/watch?v=H50jTU4vqA0 or "2012 Trailer #2" which can be found at http://www.youtube.com/watch?v=ce0N3TEcFw0.

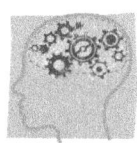

Leader Insight

Connecting to Your Students
Your students have undoubtedly heard about the predictions that the world will end on December 21, 2012. Teens are still developing the ability to think beyond the immediate future, but they are probably interested in this subject. They may have seen some of the movies about it, whether the big-budget Hollywood productions or the smaller-budget films. They may have seen some of the TV specials, whether science-based or propaganda-based.

It is likely that your students will present an apathetic face

Notes:

toward such potential dangers, but at some level they are concerned about the end of the world. They are old enough not to believe adults who say, "Don't worry; everything's going to be all right" without being offered some evidence to back up that assurance. Use this lesson to offer students a safe, non-judgmental place to voice any fears they have about this issue.

Explaining the Lesson
The idea that the world will end December 21, 2012, is based on a calendar that the ancient Mayans developed, but they didn't circle that day and write, "World ends." Pseudo-scientists have added that part, either after making unfounded assumptions or after bending the Mayan stuff to match what they already believed.

We think of the progression of years as linear: we move up a grade each year in school; we note sequential anniversaries of important days; we add "1" to the year every January first. The Mayans didn't think about time in such a linear fashion; they thought of time as running in cycles, kind of like how we view the seasons. To a farmer it doesn't really matter what year it is. What matters is that it's spring and time for planting, so the harvest will be ready by fall.

The Mayan culture thrived in and around the Yucatan Peninsula (Guatemala and southern Mexico) from about 2,000 B.C. to A.D. 250, possibly reaching a population as high as 20 million. Archeologists tell us that the Mayans were advanced, slightly ahead of most of the world at the time: developing a written language, designing and building cities with large and precisely-placed structures, using advanced mathematics, having a remarkable understanding of astronomy, but, oddly, not wheels or beasts of burden. By A.D. 900 the major Mayan cities had been abandoned. We don't know why, but speculations abound. The Spanish conquest of the area in the 1500s and 1600s destroyed most records, along with almost everybody who could interpret the few records left.

In light of this lesson, a most interesting fact about the Mayans is that they developed a calendar based on the movement of the stars. It measured 13 cycles of 144,000 days each, which totals 5,125 years. This is called the Long Count Calendar. It started on August 11, 3114 B.C., which was before the Mayans were even around. It's unknown why they started the calendar there; again, speculations abound. Cycle 13, the final cycle, of this calendar ends on December 21, 2012, if archeologists have correctly translated the few clues about understanding this calendar.

The Mayans never predicted anything other than the movement of the sun, stars, planets, and moon. Translating Mayan writings is a highly subjective endeavor, and some researchers have drawn a connection between the 2012 date and a supposed alignment between the sun, the earth, and the center of our galaxy—something that happens every 26,000 years or so. Put all this together, add a bit of imagination, and the result is that the Mayans "predicted" that on December 21, 2012, this alignment of heavenly bodies would occur, causing cataclysmic natural disasters and the end of the world.

Other cultures also have or had stories about the end of the world, including the Egyptians, the Hopi Indians, Buddhists, the Vikings, and Christians. The problem with stating a specific day, however, is that people have been saying such things for…well…always. People have always thought the world was going to end soon. Some have put an exact date on the end, and they have all been wrong. The most recent person to predict the end of the world was Harold Camping. He spent millions trying to convince everyone, and actually convinced thousands, that he had used scripture to determine that the world would end on May 21, 2011. When that day came and went and the world was still here, Camping said he'd made a miscalculation and the real date was October 21. That day, too, has come and gone. So have the 1988 and 1994 dates he predicted.

Camping is not alone. Many people have made such predictions. Hal Lindsey said the world would end by the year 2000, and before that he said we would all be gone before the 1980s were over. Benjamin Keach, a Baptist preacher, said it would be in 1689. Thomas Brightman, a Presbyterian, also thought it would happen in the late 1600s. William Miller, another Baptist preacher, said it would be March 21, 1843,…and then April 18, 1844. Since 1915, the Jehovah's Witnesses have set nine different dates, all of which have passed.

NASA says that the sun, earth, and the galaxy's center may indeed align sometime soon, but there's no way to pinpoint the exact year, much less the exact day. NASA also says there's no reason to think that this alignment will have any more effect on earth than the planetary alignments over the past few decades. People said those alignments would do all sorts of things, but they came and went with no effects on earth.

Leader Tip:
The stars and the sun, of course, don't actually move. They just look like they do because the earth is moving.

Notes:

Theological Underpinnings

The prophets of the Bible primarily spoke for God to the people about their present situation, but they sometimes spoke about future events, too. But they never offered any exact or even approximate dates for things that would happen in the future. Jesus also spoke of things to come. When Jesus spoke of the end of the world, he was decidedly vague. Once, after explaining some of the signs that would precede the day of his second coming, which is generally understood to precede the end of the world, Jesus said, "But about that day and hour no one knows, neither the angels of heaven, nor the Son, but only the Father" (Matthew 24:36).

So, anyone who says he or she knows when Jesus will return or when the world will end is claiming to know what only God knows. That's pretty arrogant. That's wanting and trying to be like God in power and knowledge rather than trying to be like God in character, which was the first sin humans committed. (See FAITH OUT LOUD, Volume 2, Quarter 1, Lesson 1, "The Fall.") Wanting and trying to be like God is the very thing that caused us to lose the perfect relationship with God, creation, and one another that God intended for us.

The opening activities should get students thinking about the end of the world, or at least the end of their own world. "Listen Up" should calm any fears about December 12. The activities in "Now What?" and "Live" affirm that life is indeed finite, and points to Jesus as the source of peace in this life and as the hope for life beyond this life.

Applying the Lesson to Your Own Life

Think back to the hysteria around the end of 1999. Not just the Y2K computer scare, but all the people saying the world would end with the new millennium. How did you react to such claims? Have you been aware of the predictions about December 21, 2012? How have you been reacting to them?

In the past there seemed to be an overarching fear for each new generation: communism, nuclear war, AIDS, random violence. Today we're dealing with multiple overarching fears all at once: random violence, global economic collapse, end of the world. How many of these fears have you seen come and go over the years? How many more do you think you'll see come and go in your lifetime? Amid all these fears, has anything steadily remained as a source of hope and peace for you?

The Lesson

Get Started (12 min.)

Video: Big Fish

Show students a scene from the movie *Big Fish*.

Warning: *In this scene a cuss word is spelled and briefly a man is shown sitting on a toilet with no nudity. If such things are offensive, skip the video and give the following verbal summary.*

In a scene from the movie *Big Fish*, a group of children sneak through the woods to visit an old lady whom they think is a witch. The rumor around town is that if you look into her glass eye you'll see how you're going to die. Some of the children chicken out and run way before even meeting the witch. Three boys remain, but only Edward is brave enough to ask the witch about her eye. The other two boys look into it. One sees himself dying as an old man and gets a little scared. The other boy sees himself dying as a young man and gets very scared. Edward says to the witch, "I was thinking about death and all. About seeing how you're going to die. I mean, on one hand, if dying was all you thought about, it could kind of screw you up. But it could kind of help you, couldn't it? Because you'd know that everything else you can survive." Edward looks into the eye, smiles, and accepts his fate with peace. Many years later as he lies in what everyone believes to be his death bed, Edward tells his adult son, with utter peace, "People needn't worry so much. It's not my time yet. This is not how I go. I saw it in the eye."

Discussion Questions:
- Would it be better to know when and how you're going to die, or would it be better to be surprised?
- Would it be better for humankind to know when and how the world will end, or would it be better for humankind to be surprised?
- What would you do if you knew the world would end in one month?

Say: *Lots of people have wondered what the end of the world will be like. There have been many movies about it. Just a few years ago, a lot of people were worried that the world would end in the year 2000.*

Notes:

 # Listen Up (20 min.)

Share with your students what you remember about the hysteria surrounding 1999 becoming 2000. Not just the Y2K computer scare, but the predictions about the world ending, or at least the threat of it becoming mostly destroyed. You may want to list some of the top-grossing movies that came out around then:

- *Independence Day* (1996)—aliens try to take over the world and destroy much of it in the attempt.
- *Twister* (1996)—tornadoes destroy a lot of stuff in Oklahoma.
- *The Fifth Element* (1997)—aliens are heading for earth to destroy it.
- *Volcano* (1997)—a volcano erupts and destroys much of Los Angeles.
- *Dante's Peak* (1997)—a volcano erupts and destroys a town.
- *Starship Troopers* (1997)—aliens attack earth.
- *Deep Impact* (1998)—a comet threatens to destroy Earth.
- *Armageddon* (1998) in which an asteroid threatens to destroy earth.
- *Lost in Space* (1998)—the earth has been rendered uninhabitable due to pollution and global warming.
- *The Matrix* (1999)—a computer secretly has taken over the earth.
- *End of Days* (1999)—the devil, on the eve of the new millennium, comes to earth to destroy it.

Discussion Question:
- What, if anything, do these movies have in common?

Note that from 2000 to 2002, after people knew that the new millennium wasn't going to bring disaster, none of the top-grossing movies dealt with the end of the world or widespread destruction. The next big disaster movie, *The Core*, didn't come out until 2003.

Ask how many of your students have seen the movie *2012*, which was released in 2009.

Show the YouTube clip entitled "Watch a 5 Minute clip from 2012 - on Blu-ray & DVD." Warning: this clip contains scenes of natural disaster and lots of people dying, but no gore. If that's too much for your class, show a trailer for the movie instead, maybe "2012 Trailer #2."

Discussion Questions:
- Does anybody think that's really going to happen before this year is over?
- If you have mostly negative answers: Is anybody a little worried that something like that might happen?
- What have you heard about the end of the world prediction for December 21?

Allow responses, and explain as much as you think is pertinent from the background material in "Explaining the Lesson." This part of the lesson will work much better as a conversation than a lecture, and the more casual the better. That means this part of the lesson may be harder to plan, as your students may have bits and pieces of factual information mixed in with some speculation, theories, and outright craziness. Try to be familiar enough with the background information to respond to the non-scientific stuff as it comes up, consulting your notes as infrequently as possible.

As students discuss, try some of these questions and comments if you need to deepen the conversation:
- Say a little more about that.
- What do most teenagers think about that? What do you think about it?
- How do most teenagers feel concerning that? How do you feel about it?
- Where is God in this?
- Where is the church in this?

You'll have to transition from conversation partner back into teacher to move from this part of the lesson to the next. If it hasn't come up already, this is a good time to assure your students that what's being presented as fact by some really isn't fact, and that many of the claims about what the Mayans said are really just people projecting their own ideas onto flimsy evidence.

Conclude this portion of the lesson with:
- As advanced as the Mayans were, and as long as they were around, their civilization pretty much disappeared over 1,000 years ago. We see this same thing happen throughout history: every civilization, every culture, no matter how great, comes to an end sooner or later. How long do you think the U.S. (Europe, Africa, Japan,

Leader Tip:
Leading this part of the lesson in a casual manner will open the door for students to be more forthright with their feelings, fears, concerns, and questions about the end-of-the-world predictions.

Leader Tip:
Even though we've studied the Mayans for several decades, the end of their calendar being associated with the end of the world only started in 1975. The idea was so unscientific that no one paid any attention to it until 1987 when somebody put it together with false data about planetary alignment. Even then, no one took it seriously until 1995 when the idea was coupled with more faulty data about heavenly alignment. Since then, though, the idea has grown in popularity.

Notes:

or another country or continent) will be around?
- The best guess is that a combination of factors wiped out the Mayans: overpopulation, depletion of natural resources, warfare, and a lack of preventative actions by leaders. What do you think might cause our civilization to collapse?
- If the U.S. disappears, how do you think that will affect Christianity?

Allow responses to this final question, but assure your students that the Christian Church is far bigger than the U.S. In fact, experts now tell us that the church is growing far faster outside the U.S. than within, especially in Central America and Africa.

Now What? (15 min.)

Say something like: *The world probably isn't going to end when humans predict it, but we never know when a natural disaster might happen. It's a good idea to be prepared by having a family plan, an emergency kit, first-aid supplies, and food and water. None of us are probably going to die anytime soon, either, but it's a good idea to be ready for that as well. We prepare ourselves for death by entrusting our lives to God through Christ.*

Then say: *Part of being prepared for a disaster is thinking ahead, having a plan. So let's spend a few minutes thinking about what each of us would do in an earthquake, flood, hurricane, tornado, tsunami, or something else that wipes out power and communication, and overburdens emergency services.*

Explain that you will read off eight choices. Students have to select one of the choices you mention and group themselves according to their choices. No sitting on the fence, making up another option, or choosing none of the above.

The choices are:
1. Stay put and pray for somebody to rescue you.
2. Search for survivors whom you might be able to help.
3. Do whatever it takes to keep other people away from the food and water you've stashed away for yourself

and your family.
4. Do whatever it takes to get food and water from somebody else.
5. Follow the plan you've made with your family and neighbors to share resources and help one another.
6. Hope to die within the first few minutes of the disaster so that you don't have to deal with the situation.
7. Let your parents worry about this. It's their job to make sure you're safe.
8. Don't plan to do anything because nothing like this will ever happen.

Once all students have made their choices and formed groups based on their answers, ask a few to explain their choices—one from each group, if you have time. Ask if anyone wants to change his or her group based on the responses.

Live It (5 min.)

Say: *As Christians, we have our own story about how the world will end. It's called Armageddon and is found in the Book of Revelation. If you had to sum up Revelation using only one word, that word would have to be: weird. You could spend the rest of your life trying to figure out what Revelation means and still only have guesses. If Revelation really is an accurate vision of "the end," then the only really important thing to know is that Christ wins.*

Say it again: *Christ wins.*

Say: *No matter when the world ends, no matter how the world ends, no matter when or how we die…if we're on Christ' side, we're on the winning side.*

Close your time together in prayer.

Resources used: *Collapse*, by Jared Diamond; Huffingtonpost.com; nasa.gov; *The New American Desk Encyclopedia*; *The Westminster Guide to the Books of the Bible*.

© 2012 Discipleship Ministry Team of the Ministry Council of the Cumberland Presbyterian Church. All Rights Reserved.

Notes:

About the contributors...

Rev. Aaron Ferry, MDiv. Memphis Theological Seminary (Nashville Presbytery), is the Associate Pastor of Christian Education at the West Nashville Cumberland Presbyterian Church. Aaron is a graduate of Memphis Theological Seminary, serves on the Discipleship Ministry Team and provides leadership for CPYC and Triennium. Aaron and his wife Mary just had their first child, Paxton, on March 30, 2012.

Samantha Hassell is a Christian Educator who has been serving the Cumberland Presbyterian Church since 2001, when she graduated from what is now Bethel University. Samantha has served congregations in both Tennessee and Kentucky and has had opportunity to serve on Presbyterial and Denominational boards and teams, as well. When God calls Samantha to do something God does so in a still small voice and, when that doesn't get her attention, with an opportunity dropped in her lap. Writing for **Faith Out Loud** was no different. Although stubborn when God calls, her love for young people and her desire to help them to grow as disciples keeps her answering, "Yes!" Samantha and her husband, Victor, have three children and serve together at Sturgis Cumberland Presbyterian Church in Sturgis, Kentucky.

Rev. Dr. Andy McClung has been teaching Cumberland Presbyterian youth and adults since 1988, both in person and through his writing. A double graduate of Memphis Theological Seminary (M.Div., 1994 and D.Min., 2002), Andy has served congregations in Alabama, Arkansas, Mississippi, and Tennessee. Cursed with a dry sense of humor and blessed with a love for the Cumberland Presbyterian Church, he lives in Memphis and continues to teach, preach, write, and serve the church at the presbyterial, synodic, and denominational levels.

Rev. Chris Warren, MDiv. Vanderbilt Divinity School (Nashville Presbytery), has served in many capacities in the Cumberland Presbyterian Church including leading music and working with youth at local, presbytery, and denominational events. He is senior pastor at the Mt. Sharon Cumberland Presbyterian Church in Greenbrier, Tennessee, where he has served since June 2008. Chris and his beautiful wife, Joy, have two wonderful children, Emma, 10, and Micah, 8.

Rev. Nathan Wheeler, MDiv. Memphis Theological Seminary (Nashville Presbytery), is the young adult minister at Tusculum Cumberland Presbyterian Church in Nashville, Tennessee. He serves on the board of the Presbyterian Student Fellowship at Middle Tennessee State University and is on the Cumberland Presbyterian young adult ministry council. Nathan recently finished and released his first eBook, *Making Love: An Exploration of the Greatest Commandment*.

Project editor is Susan Groce. Additional editing by Cindy Martin. Electronic processing and incidental layout by Matthew Gore. **Faith Out Loud** logo and cover design by Joanna Bellis. Produced for the Discipleship Ministry Team of the Ministry Council of the Cumberland Presbyterian Church.

www.ingramcontent.com/pod-product-compliance
Lightning Source LLC
Chambersburg PA
CBHW080541300426
44111CB00017B/2822